Oral History in a Wounded Country

Oral History in a Wounded Country

Interactive Interviewing in South Africa

Edited by
PHILIPPE DENIS AND RADIKOBO NTSIMANE

UNIVERSITY OF KWAZULU-NATAL PRESS

Published in 2008 by University of KwaZulu-Natal Press
Private Bag X01
Scottsville 3209
South Africa
E-mail: books@ukzn.ac.za
Website: www.ukznpress.co.za

ISBN: 978-1-86914-147-9

Managing editor: Sally Hines
Editor: Alison Lockhart
Typesetting: Patricia Comrie
Indexer: Christopher Merrett
Cover design: Flying Ant Designs
Cover photographer: Kare Ahlschwede, Germany
Cover photograph: Radikobo Ntsimane (deputy-director of Sinomlando Centre)
                interviews Florah Buthelezi on the outskirts of Nhlazatshe
                near Edendale, KwaZulu-Natal, South Africa, 16 May 2008.

Printed and bound by Interpak Books, Pietermaritzburg

Contents

Acknowledgements

This book would not have seen the light of day without the input of the programme co-ordinators, research assistants and fieldworkers of the Sinomlando Centre for Oral History and Memory Work in Africa, a research and community development centre of the School of Religion and Theology at the University of KwaZulu-Natal, whose work paved the way for this project. Particular mention should be made of Humphrey Mogashoa, James Worthington and Abraham Lieta, who contributed to the first drafts of the oral history manual currently used by the Sinomlando Centre for its training workshops.

We also need to acknowledge the financial assistance of the National Research Foundation and the Department of Arts and Culture in Tshwane (formerly Pretoria), which funded essential aspects of the common work, including the seminar held in Pietermaritzburg in May 2006 at which the authors discussed the contents of the book.

The process that led to the writing of this book was long but fruitful. A special thanks to all the authors for working tirelessly on their respective chapters and keeping all the editorial deadlines.

Lastly, we owe a word of gratitude to Tom Cannell, who read and commented on many chapters of this book, to the anonymous reviewers of the original manuscript who made very useful suggestions and to Glenn Cowley, Sally Hines and Alison Lockhart at the University of KwaZulu-Natal Press who did not spare their efforts during the last phase of the book's production.

Philippe Denis and Radikobo Ntsimane
Sinomlando Centre for Oral History and Memory Work in Africa,
University of KwaZulu-Natal

Introduction

PHILIPPE DENIS

THIS BOOK IS about oral history in South Africa. With the end of apartheid and the exciting but elusive advent of a new nation, this country is witness to the emergence of a new generation of oral historians whose aim is to develop a broader, more inclusive and culturally sensitive understanding of the South African past.

Since oral history was established as an academic discipline in the late 1940s, its methodology has been constantly refined and its theoretical assumptions questioned in South Africa as well as in the rest of the world. Even as it has developed a common professional identity through international exchanges, manifested by a definition in the *New Shorter Oxford English Dictionary*,[1] oral history remains eminently contextual. Not only do the issues raised during interviews vary from country to country, but also the interactions that take place during these interviews and the manner in which the communities concerned make sense of the memories thus collected. Textbooks such as Paul Thompson's *The Voice of the Past* or Donald Ritchie's *Doing Oral History*[2] inspired generations of oral history practitioners around the world, but because they are written for a Western audience, they do not answer all the questions asked by students, community activists and heritage workers when they collect, engage with and reflect upon oral testimonies in South Africa. It is therefore both appropriate and timeous to appraise what doing oral history in Soweto, Cape Town or Ulundi means today.

Six of the authors here, all from South Africa or long-time researchers in the country, jointly shaped the contents of this book during a seminar held in Pietermaritzburg in May 2006. Many of the contributors are members of the Oral History Association of South Africa (OHASA) and meet regularly at the conferences of this newly formed body of oral history practitioners. The Sinomlando Centre for Oral History and Memory Work in Africa, a research and community development centre of the School of Religion and Theology at the University of KwaZulu-Natal,[3] initiated and co-ordinated the project. Earlier reflection papers on oral history in post-apartheid South Africa[4] and the successive versions of a manual used since 2001 by Sinomlando to train university students, heritage workers and educators in the methodology of oral history prepared the way for the present book.

Our purpose here is to understand how the cultural, political, socio-economic and intellectual evolutions that gave birth to South Africa as we know it today affect the oral history process. This book seeks to help oral history practitioners, whether they use oral history as one technique among others to gain a better knowledge of the past, or envisage oral history as an academic discipline in its own right, to reflect critically on their practices and find better ways of handling the interview process.

Oral history and oral tradition

As Thompson points out, oral history is as old as history itself. In fact, it was the first kind of history[5] and even today, historical information continues to circulate by word of mouth, in African societies in particular. In KwaZulu-Natal, for instance, traditions concerning the Zulu royal family, or events such as the battle of Isandlwana or the Bhambatha rebellion, are preserved by traditional elders and authorised storytellers. Whether formally structured oral traditions are transmitted from generation to generation with varying degrees of distortion, as Jan Vansina and his disciples believe, or if knowledge about the past is the product of a complex network of social relationships, power struggles and mental associations, as David Cohen and the constructionist school assert, does not need to be debated here.[6] Oral history, as we understand it, is the complex interaction between an interviewer and an interviewee about events of the past, which requires questioning, as well as listening, on the part of the interviewer. This encounter shapes the story. The interview is tape-recorded and, when deemed necessary, transcribed for the use of the research community and the public at large. An oral history interview is a historical conversation, or rather, to use Ronald Grele's suggestive phrase, a 'conversational narrative'.[7]

Many scholars, social historians and anthropologists, in particular, envisage oral history as an ancillary technique of historical study, the emphasis being on the creation of historical data. The material produced through oral history research is then called oral archives. Other oral history practitioners adopt a more ambitious definition of oral history. For them, it is 'another way of doing and conceiving history'.[8] Introducing *The Voice of the Past*, Thompson intimates that oral history should 'provoke historians to ask themselves what they are doing, and why. On whose authority is their reconstruction of the past based? For whom is it intended?'[9] Oral history, in these terms, can to be seen as a 'movement'.[10] The authors of this book follow this line of thought. While recognising that oral history is often used in combination with other techniques of historical investigation to develop knowledge about the past, they see it as a fully fledged academic discipline, with the encounter between the interviewee and the interviewer at its centre.

Vansina's distinction between oral reminiscence and oral tradition is often used to distinguish oral history, a conversation between an interviewer and an interviewee based on the latter's personal reminiscences, and oral tradition, a record of past events transmitted from generation to generation.[11] Elizabeth Tonkin warns against the apparent simplicity of this distinction.[12] What, after all, is a generation? A message can pass through successive generations of tellers during the lifetime of an interviewee. What this person claims in good faith to have witnessed is, in fact, the result of a chain of transmission. On the other hand, historical information presented as oral tradition can be profoundly shaped by the personal experience and the social position of the narrator.

This discussion is of particular relevance to African communities. What makes oral history attractive in contemporary South Africa, among groups as diverse as officials in government departments, local activists and community leaders, is its perceived ability to retrieve, affirm and disseminate long-repressed African traditions. The holders of these traditions, traditional leaders, members of royal families, healers and diviners, claim to have first-hand knowledge of the community's *amasiko* (traditions), as if they were fixed objects, mechanically transmitted from generation to generation. From such a perspective, oral history and oral tradition are inseparable. Interviewing one of the community's gatekeepers – a lengthy process carried out according to a strict protocol – is meant to provide access to an unadulterated version of the ancestral traditions. Yet culture is dynamic and bearers of tradition are human agents in their own right. They select, adapt, interpret and reconstruct the cultural heritage transmitted by their forebears. In fact, the strength of a cultural tradition is its capacity to be perpetually reinvented. Oral history does not give immediate access to the most ancient traditions. It tells us how these traditions are understood and recreated in a particular community at a particular time. The purpose of an interview is to access the worldview of the interviewee with all its layers of sub-jectivity. For an oral historian, the manner in which a tradition is culturally and socially represented is no less important than the historical information provided about this tradition. Subjectivity, Alessandro Portelli notes in his classic essay, is as much the business of history as the more visible 'facts'. What the informant believes is indeed a fact just as much as what 'really' happened.[13]

A South African example may help to illustrate this point. According to an interview conducted by Mpilo Pearl Sithole with Nelson Zondi, a member of the Zondi royal family, Chief Bhambatha, the mythical leader of a failed rebellion against the poll tax in colonial Natal, succeeded his uncle, Magwababa, as chief in 1906, the year of the rebellion.[14] Contemporary documents, notably a June 1890 letter from the Secretary for Native Affairs to the Umvoti Magistrate,[15] indicate that Bhambatha was appointed in 1890 and that his uncle had been a regent and not a chief, from the death of Bhambatha's father in 1883 to the young chief's installation in 1890. Zondi's version of this historical event probably reflects an attempt by the partisans of Bhambatha to shift the blame for the many unhappy events preceding the rebellion onto Magwababa.[16] What oral history reveals in this case is that in post-apartheid South Africa, Bhambatha is portrayed as a young chief whose first – and last – act of leadership was to rebel against an unjust law.

The emergence of oral history in South Africa

Oral history as a conscious and systematic attempt to generate oral testimonies about the past through interactive interviews started with two oral history projects in South Africa in 1979. The first was initiated by the African Studies Institute of the University of the Witwatersrand, following the impetus of Charles van Onselen and some of his colleagues from the recently established History Workshop, and it focused on the life and work experiences of black peasants and sharecroppers in the Transvaal countryside.[17] The second project, developed by the Killie Campbell Africana Library and funded by the University of Natal, aimed at providing information about the domestic lives and the social, political and cultural activities of a broad cross-section of mainly isiZulu-speaking people in the Durban region.[18]

Interviewing South African people about the past was not, of course, a new idea. Long before the term 'oral history' was coined, popular writers, colonial agents, missionaries and anthropologists had started collecting oral testimonies for a better understanding of South African society. Of particular significance in this regard was the contribution of the first generation of black writers in the late nineteenth and early twentieth centuries. Sol Plaatje, for instance, provided rich portraits of Tswana history, while John Henderson Soga published a survey of the history of the isiXhosa-speaking people.[19] At the turn of the century, Magema Fuze wrote a history of the Zulu people, almost entirely based on oral testimonies, which was published in 1922 under the title *Abantu Abanyama*.[20] During the same period, countless missionaries and colonial officials gathered information about the people over whom they exercised authority, partly to understand them and partly to control them. The most remarkable of these was James Stuart, a civil servant in the Natal colonial government, who conducted and transcribed, mostly in isiZulu, hundreds of interviews between the 1890s and the 1920s.[21] With an 'amalgam of curiosity, empathy and condescending racism',[22] he created what is arguably the richest collection of oral testimonies from South African society in colonial times. Another government official who gathered oral material over a long period of time was Dr N.J. van Warmelo, chief ethnologist in the Department of Native Affairs' Ethnological Section from 1930 to 1969. He is known for having invented the 'Transvaal Ndebele' in the context of a complex dialogical relationship with indigenous intellectuals.[23] During the following decades, oral evidence continued to feature in South African academic writing, particularly by scholars investigating contemporary social phenomena, although less in the work of historians, who until the late 1970s tended to give almost absolute primacy to written documents. Oral testimony figured prominently in research into subjects such as sexuality and marriage in a Tswana chiefdom (Isaac Schapera),[24] poverty in Cape Town (Edward Batson)[25] and the effects of apartheid legislation in the Transvaal (Muriel Horrell).[26]

The emergence of oral history in the late 1970s is closely associated with the rise of a historiographical movement variously described as radical history, revisionist history, popular history or history from below. In this movement, the University of the Witwatersrand History Workshop, modelled in 1977 on a collective of the same name in England,[27] played a leading role, although academics from other tertiary institutions, in Natal and in the Western Cape in particular, were also involved. Under the influence of various and sometimes competing neo-Marxist currents of thought, the radical historians developed a new interpretation of the South African past that paid less attention to race-centred explanations than to the intricate and complex manner in which class and race had interacted to shape colonial and apartheid South Africa. The members of this movement relied heavily on neo-Marxist phraseology. Luli Callinicos, for example, insisted that the uses of oral history, folklore and popular culture should be explored 'within the paradigm of historical materialism'.[28] For those who followed the tradition of French structuralist Marxism, political economy was the key to the comprehension of the past. As noted by Vivian Bickford-Smith, this gave rise to a more coherent, but also more narrowly focused urban history, with a particular focus on African working-class formation, culture and resistance.[29] The structuralist interpretation of the past, however, was hotly contested. In the mid-1980s, a certain number of social historians started to put more emphasis on the internal dynamics of African societies and African initiatives.[30] In this attempt to move 'beyond the aridity of an unpeopled political economy to the ambiguities of everyday life', as Shula Marks puts it,[31] oral history became an important resource, as it helped to uncover the complexities of human agency.

The aim of South African radical historians was not only to rewrite the country's history. It was, in Belinda Bozzoli's words, to 'make connections between new historiographical interpretations and the increasingly radical culture of ordinary South Africans'.[32] This led the members of the movement, mainly white university-based historians, sociologists, anthropologists and literary theorists, to launch an ambitious outreach programme towards an intended audience of black and white working people, youth, students, rural dwellers and migrant workers. The History Workshop and, during a shorter period, the University of the Western Cape (UWC) People's History Project[33] invited workers, teachers and students to workshops and festivals in which popular history featured prominently. They started to visit schools, factories and working-class areas and created material to popularise their view of history.

During the 1980s, oral history had not yet reached the status of a movement in South Africa, with a professional association, a dedicated journal and a specific research agenda, as was the case in Britain and in the United States during the same period. However, significant achievements marked the development of oral history during this decade. The first was the mainstreaming of oral history in historical studies, particularly those dealing with class-formation, industrialisation and urban life in twentieth-century South Africa. In a review article published in 1990, Paul la Hausse listed at least fifteen research projects – Peter Delius on the Sekhukuneland revolt, Jeff Guy and Motlasi Thabane on the Basotho mineworkers, Philip Bonner on Basotho migrant criminal organisations, Ari Sitas on trade unionism on the East Rand and Bill Nasson on Cape Town's District Six, to name a few – that were based on oral evidence.[34] However, less use was made of oral traditions in the study of pre-colonial societies than elsewhere on the African continent. According to La Hausse, this was due to the fact that among African communities that had been radically fragmented by industrialisation, oral traditions bore traces of written history to a degree seldom encountered elsewhere in Africa.[35]

The second accomplishment was the creation of oral history projects through which hundreds of people were interviewed and their testimonies taped and transcribed. Two still exist today: the History Workshop, under the auspices of which several oral history collections have been constituted since 1979, and the Western Cape Oral History Project, created in 1985 at the University of Cape Town and renamed the Centre for Popular Memory in 2001. Others did not last as long, but collected material still accessible to researchers: the Natal University Oral History Project (1979–82), the South African Institute of Race Relations Oral History Project (1982–84), the University of Lesotho Oral History Project (1982), the Swaziland

Oral History Project (1987–90) and the Natal Worker History Project (1989–97).

No less of an achievement was the popularisation of oral history research, in schools and trade unions in particular, and the publication in popular media of life stories collected by way of interviews. Callinicos's popular volume *Working Life*, for instance, was organised around the lives of five working-class men and women.[36] *Staffrider* and *New Nation* both published similar life stories of working-class people. The People's History Open Day organised in 1987 by the UWC People's History Project with the National Education Crisis Committee included oral history workshops, mostly run by community groups and involving rural activists from the 1950s.[37] In Chapter 4, Cynthia Kros and Nicole Ulrich show how this practice has continued, in a new form, to the present day.

A shift in emphasis

The rise of radical history and, in so far as it was associated with it, oral history in South Africa can be understood as a response among left-wing intellectuals to the double movement of mass mobilisation and state repression following the 1976 Soweto uprising. During this period, all South African historians were 'caught up in the deep and narrow groove of struggle history'.[38] The events before and immediately after 1994 – the legalisation of the liberation movements, the opening of constitutional negotiations, the installation of a democratic government and the adoption of a new Constitution – drastically altered the situation. Expressions such as 'people's power' or the fight against the 'system' suddenly ceased to be self-evident. An agenda of reconstruction gradually replaced the ideal of resistance. The fall of the Berlin Wall in November 1989 and the ensuing dismantling of the Soviet Union further contributed to the crisis of the neo-Marxist ideology, which until then had had the upper hand in intellectual circles.

Among professional historians, these changes caused uncertainty and confusion. In a contribution to the *Southern African Review of*

Books, Jeff Peires commented on 'unmistakable signs of crisis and collapse' in the radical historiography in South Africa.[39] The historians' confusions, Tim Nuttall and John Wright argued, '[had] to do with the sudden evaporation, in the course of the dramatic political changes of the early 1990s, of the moral and epistemological certainties of the apartheid era'.[40]

The emergence of a new society also affected the practice of oral history and its positioning as a social and intellectual project. The most significant development was the way in which memory became the focal point of oral history studies. In the 1980s the purpose of oral history was widely seen as 'giving a voice to the ordinary people'. As Bozzoli puts it, oral history enabled scholars to 'uncover what might be otherwise hidden'.[41] Such a stance did not prevent social historians from making significant progress, through the combined use of oral and written sources, in understanding the South African past, but the methodology of oral history, the effect of interviews on personal and social development and the role of memory in creating knowledge were hardly theorised. What came gradually to be recognised in the 1990s was that an interviewee is not simply a person who transmits information about the past. How such a person relates to the interview situation also deserves attention. Oral history has the potential to help South Africans to deal with their memories of the past and build together a new sense of identity. The effect of the act of remembering on the person who remembers is at the centre of this process. In line with this understanding of memory, one of the main purposes of the Truth and Reconciliation Commission, the largest effort of collective memory ever attempted in South Africa and possibly in the world, was to heal the wounds of the past. In terms of this perspective, telling a story is more than simply producing knowledge about the past. It is — or at least has the potential to be — a life-changing event.

The same applies to the numerous oral history projects documenting 'the transition out of apartheid', to use Julia Wells's phrase in Chapter 1. In each of these projects, the past as past continues to be the focus of research. Being attentive to the effect of the interview on the interviewee does not mean that the content of the interview – in other words, what 'really' happened – does not matter. But the manner in which the story is recounted, how it is shaped by the dynamic of the interview and how it affects the interviewee's sense of identity are equally important. The past should not be seen in isolation from those who generate memories about it. Several of the authors in this book explore, from different angles, the manner in which oral history narratives bring about new understandings of the past through the interaction between an interviewer and an interviewee: Kros and Ulrich, when they discuss issues of truth and memory in school-based oral history projects in Chapter 4; Radikobo Ntsimane, who examines culture and gender in oral history in Chapter 5; Mxolisi Mchunu, as he reflects on his involvement as an oral historian interested in masculinity in his own community in Chapter 6; and Sean Field, when he examines the impact of pain and trauma on the structure of interviews in Chapter 7.

The 1990s witnessed the publication of three major works in the field of oral studies, all by authors associated with the University of the Witwatersrand. These publications developed frameworks of analysis more attentive to the complexities of the act of oral transmission than had been evident in the resistance-versus-domination paradigm of the previous decade. In *Women of Phokeng*, a study based on 22 interviews with women, Bozzoli examined how each interviewee constructed her life in a different way and how the personalities of the interviewees affected their response.[42] In '*We Spend Our Years as a Tale that is Told*', a pioneering study of oral storytelling, literacy and historical narrative in a Tswana chiefdom, Isabel Hofmeyr explained how the women she interviewed adapted to a changing social and political environment by developing appropriate narrative styles.[43] Lastly, in *The Seed is Mine: The Life of Kas Maine, a South African Sharecropper*,[44] a biography based on 60 interviews with Kas Maine and 20 interviews with members of his peer group, Van Onselen, attempting to reconstruct the history of a socio-economic category in the southwestern Transvaal during most of the twentieth century, showed his awareness of the 'knowledge transactions' taking place in the relationship between the interviewer and the interviewee.[45]

Despite such insights, South Africa remained relatively untouched by the debate raised since the 1980s in Europe and in the United States about the objectivity of the oral historian as interviewer and analyst. In the northern hemisphere, guided by the theoretical work of authors such as Grele and Portelli, oral historians became more alert to the ways in which they were affected by their interviews and how the interviewer, in turn, affected the interview relationship, the data it generated and the interpretative process and product. They turned their attention to the narrative structure of the interviews and to the process of knowledge production inherent in it.[46] It was not until the mid-1990s that two papers openly questioned the assumptions held by most South African oral history practitioners since the late 1970s. In a paper published in 1998, two history lecturers from UWC, Gary Minkley and Ciraj Rassool, criticised South African social historians for believing that by collecting oral testimonies they would gain access, almost directly, to collective memories, as if oral testimonies were always authentic and memory a simple act of transmission.[47] This framework, they argued, continued to characterise most oral history work in South Africa: 'In Johannesburg, resistance was "orally" inscribed in a process of consciousness formation by classes and individuals; in Natal, it was recorded in biography as the agency and organizational careers of ordinary people, and in Cape Town these two strands were brought together in a nostalgia of ordinary people's experience, constructed as a community splintered by state intervention.'[48] Less polemical, but no less incisive, was Carolyn Hamilton's critique of South African oral historians in a paper on oral histories and the politics of archiving.[49] One of oral historians' guiding ideas, she emphasised, was that the recording of oral histories in written form would protect sources that were otherwise in danger of being lost and that by preserving them for posterity, it would provide the underclass with continued access to their own history. The underlying assumption of this kind of vision was that only professional historians, by transcribing and publishing oral testimonies, could make them accessible to non-academic audiences: 'Relatively little work has been done to explore the extent to which "ordinary people" use history as means of thinking about the nature of the world, but it is certainly sufficient to cause us to hesitate before accepting the proposition that such activities are the special preserve of academics.'[50]

Oral history in post-apartheid South Africa

Critiques such as those of Minkley and Rassool and Hamilton highlight important issues, but by the time they were written, the intellectual practices they were addressing had already started to change.[51] In the new political context, the idea that black people needed (white) academics to write history on their behalf does not need to be refuted as much as before. A democratically elected government was in place and one of its first decisions was to appoint an arts and culture task group, which produced a 'White Paper on Arts, Culture and Heritage', recommending that a programme be set up for the transformation of heritage policies in a manner designed to correct the imbalances of apartheid history preservation and associated resource distribution and skills development.[52] Oral history, as well as song, dance and storytelling, featured prominently in this programme.[53] Whether this programme has since been implemented, first by adequate legislation, then by effective operational systems, is debated.[54] Suffice to say that the South African government – along with municipalities and various other public bodies – is one of the few governments in the world, if not the only one, to actively promote oral history in schools, museums, archives and heritage sites. Oral history is less and less the preserve of academic institutions. As highlighted by Wells in Chapter 1, a wide range of new social actors collect oral testimonies and disseminate them. In Chapter 2, Benedict Carton and Louis Vis discuss some of the methodologies that are useful in terms of these new practices of oral history, and in Chapter 3, Philippe Denis introduces the ethical protocols that are necessary to respond to the needs of South African oral history practitioners.

In the new South Africa, memory and heritage replaced popular history and history from below as central concepts in oral history studies and social history in general. 'If History Workshop dominated in the 1980s,' notes Hamilton, 'a concern with Heritage prevailed across the 1990s.'[55] The 'new, highly ceremonial form of public history' that emerged at this time, notes Alan Cobley, 'concentrated on the redemptive value of memory and of personal testimony on the one hand and on the identification and dedication of new, inclusive national monuments on the other'.[56] This trend is not specific to South Africa. A recent book on memory and methodology speaks of an 'explosion of interest in memory'.[57] All over the world, articles and monographs concerned with memory have flooded scholarly journals and academic presses and at least one new volume series is concerning itself exclusively with memory research.[58]

In the wake of the release of Nelson Mandela and the start of multiparty negotiations, a group of scholars from the University of the Witwatersrand's History Workshop started to interview former political prisoners and exiles, a project that has since been included in all state heritage policies. Between 1991 and 1994, Bonner, Delius and Barbara Harmel interviewed political leaders such as Walter Sisulu, Joe Matthews, Raymond Mhlaba, Harry Gwala and Billy Nair on their political experiences.[59] During the same period, a collection of written documents, posters, oral history tapes, videotapes and films constituted during the years of exile by the London-based International Defence and Aid Fund was relocated in the Mayibuye Centre for History and Culture at UWC. After the establishment of the Robben Island Museum, the first official heritage institution of the new democracy, in 1996, both collections were combined to form the UWC-Robben Island Mayibuye Archives, which include 2 000 oral history tapes.[60] Another state-driven memory creation initiative is the South African Democracy Education Trust (SADET), established after President Thabo Mbeki had indicated his concern about the paucity of historical material on the road to South Africa's peaceful settlement. Since September 2000, hundreds of interviews have been conducted by a team of researchers led by Bernard Magubane, a retired professor of anthropology from the University of Connecticut.[61] Extensive use of oral evidence is made in *The Road to Democracy in South Africa*, the multivolume book resulting from this project.[62] 'Written so soon after the period of its focus,' writes Thabo Mbeki in the foreword to the first volume, 'this series will have the advantage also of recording the voices of some of those who were the makers of history. Those who made the history must thus have the opportunity to participate in the process of recording that history in words, and interpret it as they see it.'[63]

In June 2002 the International Oral History Association (IOHA) held its biannual conference at the University of Natal, Pietermaritzburg, on the theme 'The Power of Oral History: Memory, Healing and Development'.[64] This gathering, which was attended by oral historians from around the world, was a milestone in the history of the international oral history movement. Meetings of South African oral history practitioners preceded and followed this event, leading to the creation of OHASA in October 2005. Following the example of the Eastern Cape Oral Studies Association created during the previous decade, provincial oral history associations were established in KwaZulu-Natal and in the Free State and Northern Cape after the IOHA conference. With the financial and logistical support of the Department of Arts and Culture and the National Archives of South Africa and its provincial counterparts, OHASA organises annual conferences that attract, alongside academics and postgraduate students, a wide range of heritage workers from national, provincial and local archives and museums. Many of the countless oral history projects launched since the turn of the century are ill equipped and struggle to reach their objectives. Their existence, however, is an achievement in itself, comparable to the popular history programmes of the 1980s. Likewise, the fact that oral history is now part of the history curriculum in South African schools gives it an importance that it never had during the years of apartheid.

A guide for oral history practitioners

This book has two aims. The first is to provide guidance to oral history practitioners, programme directors and educators who wish to start an oral history project. Carton and Vis's chapter on planning and conducting an oral history project will be particularly useful in this regard. Denis's chapter on the ethics of oral history will help oral history practitioners to understand the ethical requirements of their discipline. Kros and Ulrich's chapter, which is based on the experience of the History Workshop, discusses the problems and challenges of oral history in schools.

The second aim is to analyse aspects of oral history practice of particular relevance to South Africa. Wells's chapter, which discusses the role of oral history in post-apartheid South Africa, sets the scene. In his chapter, Ntsimane examines how culture and gender shape an interviewee's understanding of the interview process. Mchunu's chapter addresses a related issue: how oral historians engage with the communities in which they conduct research, whether or not they originally belong to these communities. Lastly, Field explores how to deal with emotional issues when doing an interview, a theme of great importance in a society affected by traumatic and violent situations.

Oral history, as Grele suggested in his groundbreaking book, is an art.[65] This art requires understanding the context of the interviewees, empathising with their emotions, being sensitive to their cultures and seeing how the interview fits in a pattern of nation development. As mentioned at the beginning of this Introduction, oral history is eminently contextual. Our ambition in publishing this book is to equip South African oral history practitioners with the skills necessary to better practise their discipline. In a country still wounded by a legacy of racial discrimination, the retrieving of oral memories is a task more urgent than ever. The challenge is to appreciate the complexity of South Africa's diverse histories, while being attentive to the dynamics of the interview and their effect on both the interviewers' and the interviewees' sense of identity. We hope that this book will contribute, however modestly, to this enterprise.

Notes

1. 'Tape-recorded historical information drawn from the speaker's personal knowledge; the use or interpretation of this as an academic subject.'
2. See Paul Thompson, *The Voice of the Past: Oral History*, 3rd ed. (New York: Oxford University Press, 2000) and Donald Ritchie, *Doing Oral History: A Practical Guide*, 2nd ed. (New York: Oxford University Press, 2003).
3. For more on the Sinomlando Centre, see http://www.sinomlando.org.za, accessed 5 May 2008.
4. See, in particular, Philippe Denis, 'Healing the Wound of the Past: Oral History in Post-Apartheid South Africa', in *Crossroads of History: Experience, Memory, Orality. XIth International Oral History Conference, Istanbul, 15–19 June 2000*, ed. Gunhan Danisman (Istanbul: Bogaziçi University, 2000), 960–65; Philippe Denis, 'Oral History in a Wounded Country', in *Orality, Literacy and Colonialism in Southern Africa* (Semeia Studies, Vol. 46), ed. Jonathan Draper (Atlanta: Society of Biblical Literature; Pietermaritzburg: Cluster Publications, 2003), 205–16.
5. Thompson, *Voice of the Past*, 25.
6. On this controversy, see Elizabeth Tonkin, *Narrating Our Past: The Social Construction of Oral History* (Cambridge: Cambridge University Press, 1992), 83–96; Carolyn Hamilton, ' "Living by Fluidity": Oral Histories, Material Custodies and the Politics of Archiving', in *Refiguring the Archive*, ed. Carolyn Hamilton et al. (Cape Town: David Philip, 2002), 209–12. The first draft of this paper was read at the International Conference of 'Words and Voices: Critical Practices of Orality in Africa and African Studies' held in Bellagio, Italy, in 1997.
7. Ronald Grele, ed., *Envelopes of Sound: The Art of Oral History*, 2nd ed. (New York: Praeger, 1991), xv.
8. Philippe Joutard, *Ces voix qui nous viennent du passé* (Paris: Hachette, 1983), 8.
9. Thompson, *Voice of the Past*, viii.
10. Ronald Grele, 'Movement without Aim: Methodological and Theoretical Problems in Oral History', in *Envelopes of Sound*, 2nd ed., ed. Ronald Grele (New York: Praeger, 1991), 127–54.
11. Jan Vansina, *Oral Tradition as History* (London: James Currey, 1985), 12–13.
12. Tonkin, *Narrating Our Past*, 87.

13. Alessandro Portelli, *The Death of Luigi Trastelli and Other Stories: Form and Meaning in Oral History* (Albany: State University of New York Press, 1991), quoted in Thompson, *Voice of the Past*, 160.

14. Mpilo Pearl Sithole, 'Genealogies of the Royal AmaZondi of Ngome', in *'Freedom Sown in Blood': Memories of the Impi Yamakhanda, An Indigenous Knowledge Systems Perspective*, ed. Thenjiwe Magwaza, Yonah Seleti and Mpilo Pearl Sithole (Thohoyandou: Ditlou Publishers, 2006), 27, 30.

15. Pietermaritzburg Archives Repository: SNA I/1/66: 760/1883, Secretary for Native Affairs to Magistrate Umvoti, 8 June 1890, quoted in Paul Thompson, 'Reconciling Recent Oral Tradition with Old Documents: Bhambatha and His Family' (paper read at the second conference of the Oral History Society of South Africa, Richards Bay, 7–10 November 2006).

16. I elaborate here on one of Thompson's comments.

17. Paul la Hausse, 'Oral Historians and South African Historians', in *History from South Africa: Alternative Visions and Practices*, ed. Joshua Brown et al. (Philadelphia: Temple University Press, 1991), 347–48, originally published in *Radical History Review* 46, no. 7 (1990): 346–56; Charles van Onselen, 'The Reconstruction of a Rural Life from Oral Testimony: Critical Notes on the Methodology Employed in the Study of a Black South African Sharecropper', *Journal of Peasant Studies* 20, no. 3 (1993): 499.

18. Killie Campbell Oral History Project Archives: AV 115–62, 165–94 and 300–448 (240 interview transcripts).

19. See Belinda Bozzoli and Peter Delius, 'Radical History and South African History', in *History from South Africa*, ed. Brown et al., 5.

20. Magema Magwaza Fuze, *The Black People and Whence They Came: A Zulu View*, trans. H.C. Lugg and ed. A.T. Cope (Pietermaritzburg: University of Natal Press; Durban: Killie Campbell Africana Library, 1979).

21. Colin de B. Webb and John Wright, eds., *The James Stuart Archive of Recorded Oral Evidence Relating to the History of the Zulu and Neighbouring Peoples*, 5 vols. (Pietermaritzburg: University of Natal Press, 1976–2001).

22. Benedict Carton, 'Fount of Deep Culture: Legacies of the James Stuart Archive in South African Historiography', *History in Africa* 30 (2003): 106.

23. William David Hammond-Tooke, 'N.J. Van Warmelo and the Ethnological Section: A Memoir', *African Studies* 54, no. 1 (1995): 119–28.

24. For more on Isaac Schapera's anthropological writings as a historical source, see Peter Delius and Clive Glaser, 'Sexual Socialisation in South Africa in an Historical Perspective', *African Studies* 61, no. 1 (July 2002): 27–54.

25. On oral evidence in the historiography of Cape Town, see Vivian Bickford-Smith, Sean Field and Clive Glaser, 'The Western Cape Oral History Project: The 1990s', *African Studies* 60, no. 1 (2001): 6.

26. Muriel Horrell, *Group Areas: The Emerging Pattern with Illustrative Examples from the Transvaal* (Johannesburg: South African Institute of Race Relations, 1966).

27. For an overview of the History Workshop's early history, see Philip Bonner, 'The History Workshop in South Africa, 1977–1994', *Journal of American History* (December 1994): 977–85. For a detailed account of how intellectual movements influenced the creation and development of the History Workshop, see Bozzoli and Delius, 'Radical History', 4–25.
28. Luli Callinicos, 'Popular History in the Eighties', in *History from South Africa*, ed. Brown et al., 263.
29. Bickford-Smith, Field and Glaser, 'The Western Cape Oral History Project', 9.
30. Bozzoli and Delius, 'Radical History', 15.
31. Shula Marks, *Not Either an Experimental Doll: The Separate Worlds of Three South African Women* (Durban: Killie Campbell Africana Library; Pietermaritzburg: University of Natal Press, 1987), 7, quoted in Alan Cobley, 'Does Social History Have a Future? The Ending of Apartheid and Recent Trends in South African Historiography', *Journal of Southern African Studies* 27, no. 3 (September 2001): 616.
32. Belinda Bozzoli, 'Intellectuals, Audiences and Histories: South African Experiences, 1978–1988', in *History from South Africa*, ed. Brown et al., 210.
33. Andre Odendaal, 'Developments in Popular History in the Western Cape in the 1980s', in *History from South Africa*, ed. Brown et al., 362–67. Launched in 1986, the People's History Project discontinued its activities the following year as a result of state repression.
34. La Hausse, 'Oral History', 343–50.
35. Ibid., 344.
36. Luli Callinicos, *A People's History of South Africa. Vol. 2: Working Life, 1886–1940: Factories, Townships and Popular Culture on the Rand* (Johannesburg: Ravan Press, 1987). See also Bonner, 'The History Workshop', 981.
37. Odendaal, 'Developments in Popular History', 366.
38. Tim Nuttall and John Wright, 'Exploring beyond History with a Capital "H"', *Current Writing* 10, no. 2 (1998): 41.
39. Jeff Peires, 'The Art of Writing History', *Southern African Review of Books* 30 (1994): 24, quoted in Nuttall and Wright, 'Exploring beyond History', 38.
40. Ibid., p. 41.
41. Belinda Bozzoli, ed., *Class, Community and Conflict: South African Perspectives* (Johannesburg: Ravan Press, 1987), 9.
42. Belinda Bozzoli, with Mmantho Nkotsoe, *Women of Phokeng: Consciousness, Life Strategy and Migrancy in South Africa, 1900–1983* (London: James Currey, 1991).
43. Isabel Hofmeyr, *'We Spend Our Years as a Tale that is Told': Oral Historical Narrative in a South African Chiefdom* (Johannesburg: Witwatersrand University Press, 1994).
44. Charles van Onselen, *The Seed is Mine: The Life of Kas Maine, a South African Sharecropper 1894–1985* (Cape Town: David Philip, 1996).
45. Van Onselen, 'The Reconstruction', 506.

46. Alistair Thomson, 'Dancing through the Memory of Our Movement: Four Paradigmatic Revolutions in Oral History' (paper presented at the fourteenth conference of the International Oral History Association, Sydney, July 2006).

47. Gary Minkley and Ciraj Rassool, 'Orality, Memory and Social History in South Africa', in *Negotiating the Past: The Making of Memory in South Africa*, ed. Sarah Nuttall and Carli Coetzee (Cape Town: Oxford University Press, 1998), 89–99. An earlier version of this paper was presented with the title 'Oral History in South Africa: Some Critical Questions' at the Centre for African Studies, University of Cape Town, on 22 March 1995. See also Nicole Rousseau, 'Popular History in South Africa in the 1980s: The Politics of Production' (Master's thesis, University of the Western Cape, 1994).

48. Minkley and Rassool, 'Orality, Memory and Social History', 93–94.

49. Hamilton, '"Living by Fluidity"', 209–27.

50. Ibid., 216.

51. Bickford-Smith, Field and Glaser, 'The Western Cape Oral History Project', 16.

52. Department of Arts and Culture, 'White Paper on Arts, Culture and Heritage' (1996). http://www.dac.gov.za/white_paper.htm, accessed 4 June 2007.

53. Ibid., Chapter 5.2: 'Attention to living heritage is of paramount importance for the reconstruction and development process in South Africa. Means must be found to enable song, dance, story-telling and oral history to be permanently recorded and conserved in the formal heritage structure.'

54. For a critical assessment of current heritage policies, see Carolyn Hamilton, 'Emerging Themes and Trends, Opportunities and Challenges' (concluding paper of a workshop organised by the South African History Workshop and the Rosa Luxemburg Foundation, Johannesburg, 16–18 November 2006), http://www.public-conversations.org.za/pdf/archival_platform_paper.pdf, accessed 4 June 2007.

55. Ibid.

56. Cobley, 'Does Social History have a Future', 618.

57. Suzannah Radstone, 'Working with Memory: An Introduction', in *Memory and Methodology*, ed. Suzannah Radstone (Oxford and New York: Berg, 2000), 1.

58. The Routledge series: *Studies in Memories and Narrative*. The first volume was published in 1998. Fourteen titles have appeared so far.

59. See Bernard Magubane, Phil Bonner and Noor Nieftagodien, 'The Turn to Armed Struggle', in *The Road to Democracy in South Africa, Vol. 1: 1960–1970*, South African Democracy Education Trust (Cape Town: Zebra Press, 2004), 54 and *passim*.

60. See http://www.robben-island.org.za/departments/heritage/mayibuye/mayibuye.asp, accessed 5 June 2007.

61. See http://www.sadet.co.za, accessed 5 June 2007.

62. See South African Democracy Education Trust, *The Road to Democracy in South*

Africa, Vol. 1: 1960–1970 (Cape Town: Zebra Press, 2004); South African Democracy Education Trust, *The Road to Democracy in South Africa, Vol. 2: 1970–1980* (Pretoria: University of South Africa Press, 2006).

63. Ibid., *Vol. 1*: ix.
64. Philippe Denis and James Worthington, eds., *The Power of Oral History: Memory, Healing and Development. XIIth International Oral History Conference, Pietermaritzburg, 24–27 June 2002*, 4 vols. (Pietermaritzburg: Sinomlando Centre, 2002).
65. Grele, ed., *Envelopes of Sound.*

1

Are We Nation-Building Yet?

The Role of Oral Historians in Documenting the Transition out of Apartheid

JULIA WELLS

ORAL HISTORIANS WORKING in South Africa have an unprecedented opportunity to contribute to the documentation of one of the world's most significant transitions. The apartheid policy of the past, prescribing strict racial segregation at every possible turn, was branded a 'crime against humanity' by the United Nations and the iniquities of the policy were frequently compared to the Holocaust by the rest of the world. The advent of democracy in 1994 marked an abrupt reversal of South Africa's image and the country came to be seen as a world leader in the arts of peace-making, reconciliation and the championing of human rights. But South Africa's global reputation and the actual daily experiences of people living here are not the same thing. Furthermore, the evolution of experiences, values and dominant social attitudes has been very rapid and extremely complex.

The nature of oral history work offers its practitioners a special opportunity to document the changes because it self-consciously links past and present. The act of interviewing takes place in the present and so is fundamentally shaped by what both the interviewer and the interviewee are experiencing in their daily lives. Yet the content of what is shared involves remembering and interpreting the past. A good oral historian needs to be fully alert to the ways in which these two dynamics interact with each other, which demands sensitivity and nuanced thinking. Ultimately, it is the oral historian who will package the knowledge gained from interviews for presentation to wider audiences, and hence it is important for him/her to have a sense of the dynamics of change and evolution that the informants may be reflecting. This chapter aims to identify some of the key parameters of understanding the process of change in South Africa, as well as to raise a number of questions designed to reveal and interrogate how we think about our work as oral historians.

In the post-apartheid period, re-exploring and using our understandings of the past has become an important concern. As mentioned in the Introduction, the practice of oral history has moved out of classrooms and universities and is used by a wide range of people in community groups and by those in pursuit of government-driven programmes. The government itself has embraced rigorous and creative uses of information about the past in a number of ways and has set the pace through policy statements and investments in numerous heritage-related institutions and programmes. Under-pinning such initiatives is a core assumption that these efforts all relate to nation-building, which implies a deliberate effort to construct something that did not previously exist. The functions of oral historians, as an important component of the wider heritage sector, logically fall under this banner.

However, the title of this chapter refers to a common joke. When children are travelling with their well-intentioned parents on a family holiday, there comes a time when they ask, 'Are we having fun yet?' The question implies that the answer is not yet clear. Something feels as if it is missing. By asking the question, it is clear that the task of nation-building is not yet finished and this deserves reflection in order to assess the status of this process.

What is meant by the term 'nation-building'? Broadly stated, it implies the creation of a new sense of national identity, which will be constructive, positive and promote high levels of social cohesion. These things are seen as necessary to hold together a country that was so deeply divided in the past. Although this is an extremely broad concept, a few key ingredients lie at its centre. These include all efforts to dispel the power of racially based thinking and practices, finding ways to address the pervasiveness of poverty and inequality, and working towards redress of past injustices. The work of oral historians in southern Africa today cannot avoid touching on some aspect of these issues in one way or another and the sense that working with the past must make things different and better sets South Africa apart from other countries.

As oral historians record the stories told during this period of transition, they face an exciting, but complex task. A transition is an intermediate phase, somewhere between the past and the future. Oral history is a specialised craft, which requires that practitioners have a detached overview of the historical period and the agents or subjects of that history. In documenting the transition, therefore, one must know as much as possible, not only about the past, but also about the present. Furthermore, some kind of future ideal gives guidance as to where a society is heading. No matter how distant a future post-racial order might appear to be, its imagined characteristics can help us to assess where we are in the present. It helps to have a vision of a radically different future. What would it mean to live in a fully post-racial world? Can we imagine the dynamics and the emotions? What if all the negative aspects of racism, colonialism and imperialism had run their course? An important way to help in ushering in a new vision is to see racism as an aberration in the human experience. By putting it in its rightful place, its hold over people is diminished. If it had an unhealthy beginning, and can be seen as some sort of disease or plague that infected the human race (for a few centuries), it becomes possible to get back to 'normal', for it to come to an end. If it was an aberration, there must be evidence of how the world might have functioned without it. Are these the goals people are striving for? How close have they come to achieving them?

The role of race in understanding the past
Although South Africa is well into its second decade of democracy, race can still be used as an effective analytical tool for measuring the

major social transitions because of its centrality in defining the past. Ideally, at some still distant future point, it will feel outdated and irrelevant. For now, it still impacts on the social fabric in several major ways. First, South Africans live in a world in which many aspects of the racially defined past remain stubbornly in place. For the vast majority of South Africans, residential patterns, social mixing and access to economic and educational resources have not changed. Suspicion, distrust and alienation from people of different racial backgrounds are still common. The historian might well ask a number of related questions: Why are certain legacies so hard to root out? What efforts have been made to remove them? Why are some practices and beliefs so resilient to change, despite well-intentioned efforts?

Second, it is important to consider the subtle and perhaps unconscious ways in which the apartheid legacy informs current social issues. As race consciousness fades from our minds, it is replaced by other serious social problems. For example, what role does the apartheid legacy play in the way in which the HIV/AIDS pandemic flourishes and has been handled by the government? Surely the system of migrant labour, rooted in the apartheid Bantustans or so-called homelands, played a significant role in creating deep-rooted attitudes towards casual sex and multiple partners? Thus the racial structuring of South African society in the past still has an impact on issues that are not strictly racially determined, such as the spread of a disease.

Third, some contemporary social ills may well be troubling by-products of the rapid post-1994 transition itself. The legal foundation of the new democracy developed within a context of intense struggle that produced leaders of enormous moral integrity, such as Nelson Mandela, Archbishop Desmond Tutu and Oliver Tambo. The Constitution is the product of a creative collective commitment to rectify all the wrongs of the dying apartheid system. Many men and women rallied to the challenge and produced numerous additional policy guidelines in the form of White Papers, which in turn informed legislation in all sectors. As laudable and as necessary as this was, it also had the effect of generating policies that were top-down, at times articulating values that were not necessarily widely understood or shared by ordinary people. A prime example of this is in the arena of gender relations. The Constitution prescribes full and equal rights for all. However, the frightening level of abuse of women and children suggests the possibility of a backlash from men who are unwilling or unable to accept shifts in power relations within the home and broader society. In a more general way, it might be said that the high levels of crime in South Africa are the by-product of a heightened sense of entitlement, which may be a result of expectations in the new democracy. Similarly, many political leaders have succumbed to opportunistic grabbing of positions, or to corruption, perhaps stemming from a sense of being owed something for their past suffering. All these examples are symptoms of people who are not coping with change.

Another trend to take note of is the emergence of neo-apartheid thinking, in which old attitudes resurface, but are now practised by blacks, instead of whites. This includes attacks on press freedom, actions that intimidate people from enjoying freedom of speech, the return to a culture of control through fear, blatantly differential treatment along racial lines to exclude non-blacks from government programmes and benefits, playing upon ethnicity and culture as a way of drawing exclusionary boundaries and measuring a person's employability by their degree of adherence to politically correct principles. The dynamics of the abuse of power need to be understood as not being limited to people of one racial group or another.

Finally, oral historians need to be alert to times, places and experiences when it feels as if genuine change has taken place and formerly commonplace racial attitudes have disappeared or become marginal. The growth of the black middle class, the integration of schools and neighbourhoods, and improving interpersonal relationships are all part of the transition. How has this happened and what factors were present to create such situations? The act of documenting positive instances of change can assist in creating awareness of gains that have been made.

All of these trends and tendencies operate simultaneously as part of the transition from apartheid to democracy. The oral historian's task of knitting together the events of the past and the present can play an important role in clarifying the dynamics of change and helping to make sense out of a potentially perplexing world. With the advent of democracy, South Africa set itself on a course designed to overcome the racist legacy it inherited. Few would dispute that the hopes and dreams of a happy rainbow nation have not yet fully materialised, but the fundamental goals and targets for the future remain a powerful force that gives direction and meaning to the transition, no matter how bumpy or slow the ride is.

Stages of evolution in uses of historical knowledge

As South Africa moved away from its apartheid legacy, a variety of approaches to making use of the historical past evolved in quick succession, including both government initiatives and academic practices. To date, five different phases can be identified. It needs to be understood, however, that these phases do not have fixed starting and stopping points. Rather, each one represents shifting levels of awareness, focus and attention. Therefore, the ideals and thinking of one phase continue and overlap with the next one, much like the waves of the ocean, which are both coming and going at the same time.

It is useful for oral historians to be aware of the changes in order to see where their initiatives and projects fit into the larger whole. They also need to have a sense of the range of ideas and contexts that might affect what their informants are saying, as well as to appreciate what potential funders and other participants might be looking for in a project. What follows is a simple chronology of the stages in the evolution of post-apartheid uses of the past in South Africa to date, which can also be seen as different stages in nation-building.

Anti-apartheid phase

This phase includes what was inherited from the immediate apartheid past at the time of the first democratic elections. Most things to do with history and the past were associated with the political use of history as a tool of propaganda by the apartheid state. Heritage institutions, such as museums and monuments, all reflected the values of white supremacy and the exclusion or marginalisation of the black majority. History had a bad name and was seen as offensive by many because of its expropriation as an instrument of apartheid policies and as a means of exclusion.

On the other hand, as outlined in the Introduction, a number of universities around South Africa had started oral history programmes designed to augment the struggle against apartheid. These projects included the key elements of giving a voice to the voiceless and designing multifaceted educational and community outreach programmes to ensure that the historical knowledge gained from oral history projects reached a wider audience. The apartheid government considered many such projects subversive, but they were to form the basis of the newly evolving heritage practices in the 1990s, when such approaches became widely accepted and championed by the new government.

As change swept South Africa in the early 1990s, the first response in the heritage sector was to invert all the negative aspects of its abuses under the apartheid government. To a certain extent, this can best be understood by looking at the values and dynamics that underscored the struggle: whatever apartheid stood *for*, the fighters for freedom were *against*. This included using race as an excuse to subordinate others, the grossly uneven distribution of state resources and violations of basic human rights. Dismantling all the negatives of the apartheid system was at the top of the agenda. An important part of this process was the establishment of the legal framework to end all forms of discrimination, with the Constitution standing as a key pillar in constructing a new sense of fairness as the prevailing national ideology.

Reconciliation phase

This phase is often associated with the presidency of Nelson Mandela. As the new nation emerged, it needed to offer reassurance to itself and to the rest of the world that it was dedicated to a totally different kind of moral order. This included finding ways of managing the still raw tensions and pains of the immediate past. The tone and image of the new South Africa were set at this stage. One of the priorities was to reassure white South Africans that their future was safe under majority rule. The government wanted to avoid outbreaks of violence or large-scale 'white flight', but also wanted the black population to feel hopeful and confident that legitimate anger and outrage at past injustices would be dealt with.

During this era, a new flag and national coat of arms and new public holidays were introduced as ways of using the symbols of the historical past in a constructive and unifying way. By now, these are familiar and the complexity of their meanings and messages may be lost on the younger generation. The Truth and Reconciliation Commission fits into this phase, providing a vivid witness to the ways in which oral testimony can be used to assist in the healing and recovery process. Both victims and perpetrators of the most offensive crimes and human rights abuses committed under apartheid told their stories to the cameras of the world, bringing to light many buried truths. The focus on reconciliation covered roughly the mid-1990s.

Reconstruction phase

From the mid- to the late 1990s, a new zeal for developing policies and frameworks for all sectors emerged. Plans were laid to begin the hard work of trying to transform the fundamental infrastructure of the nation, including the backlog in housing, jobs, education, basic services and governance skills. Delivery of tangible social services topped the list of government priorities.

In the heritage sector, two key developments emerged. The first was to try to address some of the inherited racial imbalances by placing people of colour in heritage institutions and leadership roles. New monuments, museums and exhibitions were also created in order to capture themes and content of greater relevance to the black majority. In recognition that this amounted to somewhat superficial window dressing, without affecting the fundamental nature of heritage practice, the government developed a 'White Paper on Arts, Culture and Heritage' in 1996. Although seen today as perhaps a little too heavily influenced by international expertise, this policy document did establish the important principle of the government's maintaining an arm's-length approach to arts and culture. The intention was to ensure that freedom of creativity and expression could be enjoyed freely by all people, and to avoid the use of these sectors for propaganda by the government.

During this phase, the government poured large amounts of money into large, new projects, such as the Robben Island Museum, and established a list of further so-called legacy projects to be built over time. These all focused on honouring aspects of the struggle against apartheid and its special heroes. The policies that defined the creation of the South African Heritage Resources Agency and the National Heritage Council were written during this phase. Also during the late 1990s, the private sector began investing in large heritage projects, such as the Apartheid Museum in Johannesburg. This phase marks the growth of viewing the heritage sector as significant, with potential financial pay-offs. Using the past to construct a different future began to play an important role in nation-building.

African Renaissance phase

This phase is often associated with the start of Thabo Mbeki's presidency in 1999, as he became a strong advocate of promoting African achievements in all spheres. This resulted in a fresh appreciation of the intangible aspects of heritage, such as oral history, oral traditions, cultural expressions and indigenous knowledge. The Mbeki government sponsored the creation of Freedom Park near Pretoria, designed to serve as a space for spiritual renewal and also as a museum and monument to eight different struggles for freedom in

South African history. In its conception, this marked a shift away from a narrow focus on the anti-apartheid freedom struggle, towards a more intangible focus on freedom more generally. Funding became available for scientific research into indigenous knowledge systems through the National Research Foundation and, later, the Department of Science and Technology. The government designated the National Archives to manage oral history development.

Unlike the earlier phases, this was not about appeasing whites, nor was it simply a case of putting African content into intrinsically Eurocentric institutions. It shifted the focus to creating and utilising new forms of knowledge in new ways. This included an awareness of the need to change mindsets – perhaps the hardest part of nation-building. This is something that cannot be forced or measured, but without it, any other changes fall short of truly making a difference. New mindsets are about a fundamental paradigm shift, not just a patching up, catching up or equalising. However, most of the initiatives of this phase remained somewhat elitist and top-down, initiated by the government.

Democratisation phase

In this phase, which could be said to have started in the first few years of the twenty-first century, involvement and interest in finding new ways to use the past creatively for the basic goals of nation-building began to be embraced by ever wider numbers of people. There was a virtual explosion of community-based heritage projects, with new ideas for projects emerging at all levels. The launch of the National Heritage Council in 2004 helped to accelerate this trend, as the organisation held a number of consultative conferences throughout the country, highlighting the new possibilities of the sector and spreading awareness. The Council then developed a funding programme, making it easier for a wide range of local initiatives to get vital financial support.

This phase marked an important shift in all aspects of heritage work from museums and universities to the world outside of such traditional institutions. In many cases, it was these very institutions that championed outreach efforts, devising a variety of creative ways to engage with the communities beyond their walls. With this shift also came a new emphasis on using aspects of heritage for economic development, primarily through tourism, but also in arts, crafts, performance and training programmes. Democratisation also found expression in youth projects and community health projects, such as the Sinomlando Centre for Oral History and Memory Work in Pietermaritzburg, which helps orphans from the HIV/AIDS pandemic to remember their personal legacies and heritage.

Points of intersection

From the brief descriptions above, the overlapping nature of the phases can be readily understood. An example might be a project that is currently being funded in the democratisation phase, yet focuses on oral history related to a local monument that was built in the reconstruction phase to honour struggle heroes, while being designed to promote reconciliation and to create jobs in the tourism sector. Contemporary projects might reflect the values of the democratisation phase, but deal with content that was common during earlier phases. None of the goals of each phase have been fully completed to date and all can be considered as still valid for further examination and development.

Healing tools of oral historians

The work of oral historians and all heritage practitioners involves deeply understanding the continuum from the depths of racial oppression in the past to a radically different mindset that will characterise the future. A sense of movement in the way that society thinks gives new perspectives on the past and helps to deflate the seemingly endless negative power of racially based thinking. Perhaps the greatest injustice of all during the period of racial thinking was the extent to which people of all races internalised beliefs in both racial superiority and inferiority.

The stories told by people who are interviewed today will reveal where they are on their own personal journeys towards recovery and wholeness. In recording an interview, the oral historian documents this process in a way that allows the story to be used for a deeper analysis. Highly skilled oral historians understand that their role extends beyond simply recording the testimonies of others. The interview itself is a specially created safe space for an intimate dialogue, very often focusing on topics that fall outside of everyday experiences and conversations. The interviewer determines what will be discussed and the kinds of questions asked, and it is arguable that he/she becomes a co-creator of knowledge relating to the larger nation-building agenda. The very process of practising oral history contributes to creating the transition, so it should be practised with great wisdom and insight. However, the benefits of interviews are not for historians alone. Very often the informants feel great relief and release from having had someone listen to their life stories. Both forms of healing – individual and social – form part of the mandate of nation-building. Oral research methodology can achieve this in a number of ways:

1. It is still important to name the offences, to document the sins, crimes and injustices of the past. The mere act of bringing them to light defuses people's pain and allows for letting go. It helps people who suffered to know that they are not marginalised or forgotten and it allows others to offer support.
2. Our efforts can expose the flimsiness of racism as an artificial construct, premised on lies, distortions, fear and greed. Knowing where destructive practices and thinking come from helps to bring them down to size. Their power and influence can then be more easily discarded from our contemporary mindsets.
3. Good research can find many stories of people and conditions that were not strictly dictated by racially based thinking. If left to their own devices, without the coercion of dominant institutions, people of all races in the past could act in simple,

fair and humane ways. They may have been seen as aberrations at the time, but their stories assist us to demythologise any sense of inevitability in the racially constructed past. For example, a few black students were totally transfixed by reading Hazel Crampton's book *The Sunburnt Queen*,[1] which describes how, over many decades, shipwrecked Europeans were adopted and incorporated into Xhosa society along the southeast coast of Africa. The students said they just could not stop telling their friends about these stories, to the point of becoming obsessive. For them, the knowledge that even a few Europeans had in fact come to Africa and fully assimilated to become Africans, through marriage and adoption of cultural practices, was mind-boggling. Just imagine, they said, a world in which Europeans did not or could not practise their superiority complexes! It did exist.

4. Researchers face the massive task of unearthing the vast number of human experiences that were buried or margin-alised in the past. Racially defined histories and knowledge systems are being overtaken today by attention to neglected histories and the retrieval of indigenous knowledge systems. So part of the healing lies in achieving equity in our entire base of knowledge.

5. Our work also frequently takes the form of retelling old stories in new ways and from new perspectives. For example, in Grahamstown, township tour guides take visitors first to the top of the ridge from which a major attack in 1819 was launched by the amaXhosa. This allows the visitors to engage with the hope and determination of the warriors and the sense of justice they must have felt in trying to reclaim their land, rather than focusing on the bloodshed in the valley below, where their defeat lost them their claim to huge parts of the Eastern Cape. For the young guides, the story is less about defeat than it is about the determination and bravery of their ancestors to achieve justice.

6. Oral history work can result in helping to transform the physical landscape around us. A new understanding of the past can find material expression in monuments, murals, exhibitions and new buildings, or even new art forms. These in turn become part of the transformed realities of the future.

It is not unusual for oral historians see people experience glimpses of new ways of seeing and being in the course of their work. To put it in psychological terms, many oral historians have witnessed 'Aha' moments – when a major conceptual breakthrough takes place. This is what makes our work so gratifying. The essence of those exciting moments often has to do with healing that comes from a shift in consciousness, and more often than not, a shift that involves a higher level of self-understanding. People *are* discovering new ways of seeing their roles in the world they live in. But what is it that is being seen?

Documenting the transition

If oral historians are to document the period of transition, what kinds of questions should they be asking? Where do they find evidence of the extent to which people are moving towards less racially based ways of thinking and a new liberated consciousness, or remaining stuck in the negative legacy of the past? This section suggests a number of questions that might assist in evaluating the process unfolding around us. Practitioners will no doubt develop many more in the course of their work.

Are people maintaining or dropping racially based analytical categories?

To assess this question, one needs to observe the extent to which racial stereotypes are still being invoked as explanations for things happening as they did in the apartheid past. The healthier alternative is an awareness of how dehumanising systems of thought and government operated, shifting blame from cruel individuals to cruel institutions. This leaves room for the institutions to die and for the individuals to reform.

What are the differences in the present between public and private spaces and activities?

As noted earlier, the transition to a democratic Constitution and a non-racial legal framework took place in the early post-apartheid period. However, the intentions of the law and how people live their private lives are two different matters. Legal equality does not translate directly into the transformation of social habits, so within the sphere of the private, racial separation is most often still found to be the dominant practice.

What do ethnic identities mean to people and why do they have this meaning?

For centuries, the Eurocentric colonial mindset tried to impose the notion that ethnicity explained everything. In a world of competing values, vast differences in access to economic resources and great threats to physical survival, ethnicity offered a blanket of comfort, evoking a sense of kinship, family and security. Given the intimate and personal nature of ethnic identity, it is not surprising that it is still highly valued by many people. Often, strenuously affirming the strong points of one's ethnicity served to counteract the allegations of inferiority that came with the colonial package. In South Africa today, ethnicity remains a cherished commodity. Yet some of the forces of globalisation and nation-building pull in the opposite direction, placing ever greater emphasis on the shared and universal aspects of our human make-up. How people cope with these tensions is a very important part of the story of transition.

What are the changing relationships between race and power?

In this transition period, the voting power of the black majority operates within the context of economic power remaining in the hands of a white minority. The role of the government in supporting, or not, the demands of the working class, which voted it into power, has to be weighed against the interests of those who pay the bulk of the taxes. How do these two powerful forces balance each other?

Are predominantly white business interests impeding social and economic development? How are these dynamics experienced by people on the ground?

How does a national identity function in relation to group identities?

Of course, all people live with multiple identities. What needs to be documented is the relative importance assigned to each one. In our search for the emerging new nation, it is important to assess how these values might be shifting and changing. Are there moments where a course of action might be decided based on the wider national good, instead of on the more familiar and comfortable alignment with a narrower, ethnic identity?

How do people relate to the government?

The relationship of people to the state is one of the key areas of difference in the new South Africa. What affects people's decisions to either participate in or withdraw from state-initiated activities? While the state has articulated its non-racial, non-sexist goals within a dominant international human rights discourse, it is important to know how this is actually being experienced by ordinary South Africans. What affects decisions to either buy in or to opt out? What influences decisions to support or sabotage? Is the state perceived as an enemy or as a vehicle of transformation?

The craft of oral historians in capturing the transition

If an oral history project is going to assist with any of the goals of nation-building, this needs to be understood and incorporated into the planning of a project from the beginning. First, it is important to prioritise the task of documenting the transition from the very first stages of conceptualising a project, which will assist in the formulation of clear targets, hoped-for outcomes, informants to be sought and questions to be asked.

Second, despite commitments to objectivity and being neutral, oral historians know that the very practice of talking to people also leads and guides informants in certain ways. Many practitioners have experienced the healing, liberating dynamics of conducting oral interviews, when the very nature of their questions creates opportunities for reflection in an original way. At times oral historians experience situations where an informant says something like, 'Well, I never thought of it that way, but . . .' and then goes on to recall vibrant and useful stories. In this way, a self-conscious exploration of the nation-building questions can lead and guide people into understanding their own lived experiences in new ways.

Third, oral historians need the 'big-picture framework' to assist in performing an analysis and evaluation of the information that is gathered. They need to be a little God-like, having an almost omniscient view of what is learned and the context from which it comes. They need to be able to decode the hidden meanings in certain words, actions and symbols, as well as to analyse what is remembered and what is forgotten, and why. The oral historian's own intelligence and experience forms an essential part of the process of generating new knowledge.

And finally, many oral historians today prefer to remain actively engaged with their findings, right through to the final design of documentation that allows the new insights to be fully shared with the public. This has become more possible in the context of the democratisation of the heritage sector, with its emphasis on practical applications. Performances, exhibitions, wall murals and other works of art can all convey the messages far more vividly than simply using printed words. The advantage of these types of applications is that they often transcend differences in literacy levels, as well as language barriers in a multilingual society. Knowledge and insight that merely sit on library shelves do not serve anyone beyond a very narrow circle. It is part of the nation-building dynamic that the widest possible audiences and uses should be sought as the destination of oral historians' efforts.

Obstacles to the new vision

Having a vision of a deracialised future assists in our analysis of the dynamics of transition, but the problems and obstacles in achieving it need to be honestly and frankly assessed and incorporated into the work of oral historians. It is important to understand what forces act against achieving a truly different kind of social order and collective mindset. The present conditions seriously affect both the interviewer and the interviewee in how they see things and a variety of forces are currently operating to contain and constrain positive change. These factors should be documented by those wishing to understand the complexity of the South African transition.

What will historians of the future be able to know and say about the times we are now living in? How is the contest between reactionary and progressive forces evolving? One of the greatest threats to genuine transformation and nation-building is the very real possibility of leaving racially built systems of inequality in place, while simply replacing white faces with black ones. The new black elite may be judged as having done all in its power to secure the same privileges for itself as its white predecessors. If this is the case, class privilege will simply replace racial hierarchies and deep social and economic inequalities will never be effectively addressed.

Globalisation also presents powerful constraints on the achievement of the new South African vision. Deeply rooted economic forces on a macro-level may not allow for a fundamental restructuring of the economic order. Furthermore, the personal mindsets associated with the still dominant northern hemisphere economies may ride roughshod over the South African dream of spreading *ubuntu*, sharing and humanity. Consumerism, careerism and individualism offer potent challenges to the core goals of nation-building and, in this way, they are akin to the racism that the nation is trying to move away from.

Furthermore, the move into a common, shared sense of nationhood may trigger a backlash from people who have a great fear of a loss of identity. Insecurity on a deep personal level can often lead to strange forms of social behaviour. This profound fear of change is conservative in nature, but can be found among people of all ethnic groups.

There is no doubt the greatest obstacle of all is the sheer

magnitude of poverty in South Africa. Enjoying a sense of well-being about a new national identity is a luxury that is not available to people still struggling with issues of basic survival. The old-fashioned class struggle of the have-nots against the haves will not be eliminated until economic justice has been achieved. While it may be argued that a positive mindset can provide a crucial tool for elevating oneself in life, this should not be exaggerated or overrated. Genuine 'decolonisation of the mind' (to use Ngugi wa Thiong'o's evocative phrase) cannot take place without some genuine and concrete decolonisation of people's lived daily experience.

A closely related phenomenon that oral historians would do well to take note of is the role of a culture of expectations. In a time of glowing hopes and promises, it may be that expectations will outstrip the capacity of the government to deliver. This, too, can be an important cause of instability. How is it being negotiated? How are failures and achievements being perceived? These are the kinds of questions oral historians could be asking.

In the battle to eradicate poverty and to manage expectations, the youth offer something of a wild card. On the one hand, they are freer of the racially based baggage of the past than their elders and can move more quickly in new directions. On the other hand, if they feel shut out of the economy and hopeless about their own prospects, they might well be in the forefront of the revolutions of the future. All of these dynamics can threaten the nation-building agenda and reveal important social phenomena in the current historical moment and are worth documenting.

Conclusion

The mandate of the nation-building challenge is to find ways of affirming people's full humanity, releasing and retrieving all that has been suppressed by the racial discourse that has dominated South Africa for so long. This humanity has always been there, but now it is being documented, celebrated and shared in virtually unlimited ways. As South Africa makes a collective transition out of apartheid, it is inevitably involved in a process of change in which the outcomes are unparalleled, but hard to predict. This lends a sense of urgency to the work being undertaken by oral historians, who are in a rare and privileged position to capture, document and share what is, by all accounts, a very dramatic story.

Part of the nature of a transition is that both the past and the future operate simultaneously. People are all moulded by their pasts, but have a sense of where they are heading. During such a time, everyone lives with coexisting realities. At times it feels as if nothing has changed and as if it never will; at other times, one is left breathless by the realisation that something profound has shifted and we will never go backwards. Sometimes individuals move from one reality to another within a matter of minutes, needing to shift mental gears on a moment-by-moment basis. South Africans live simultaneously in a world that is still fully defined in racial and ethnic terms, while at times they also find themselves functioning in a way that knows no bounds, where the common features of being human are all that matters. For now, it is important to be able to read the signals and constantly adapt. In an ideal world, people would be able to embrace different aspects of their multiple identities as easily as changing coats to suit each shift in the weather.

Oral historians are challenged to become expert reality detectors. Awareness of the dynamics of the transition period can inform the way in which projects are structured. Then, once in the intimate space of the interview situation, the oral historian needs to be able to intuitively understand how the multiple layers of the past, present and future are being articulated. What reality are informants operating out of? In which phase of the evolutionary process of nation-building do their various stories and memories belong? What are they telling you about their own journey? How is the nation-building happening? What are the obstacles?

At some point in the future, the transition will be considered finished. Just imagine a time when the job of trying to define African experience as equal to European is done – when no one questions it, or even cares about it anymore! Imagine that the indigenous knowledge of Africa is known, shared, used and treasured by everyone on the planet. Imagine that all the hidden histories have been celebrated as public treasures and all the unsung heroes and heroines have been honoured. Imagine that all the stories of journeys from despair to prosperity have been told – then the oral historians can rest.

Note
1. Hazel Crampton, *The Sunburnt Queen* (Johannesburg: Jacana, 2004).

2

Doing Oral History[1]

BENEDICT CARTON AND LOUISE VIS

EXPERIENCED ORAL HISTORIANS emphasise different approaches to starting a project, but most agree that the early planning stages should focus on formulating a clear topic that integrates planning, the collection of data, interpretation, write-up and preservation.[2] This methodological process should prompt researchers to contemplate the rewards and challenges of fieldwork. Undergraduate projects, for example, could lead to other academic opportunities. Many South African BA Honours theses based on oral history have become MA or Ph.D. dissertations. Yet future benefits should never overshadow ethical responsibilities and logistical concerns. For example, researchers cannot simply identify any person as a major contact.[3] In South Africa, as elsewhere, contacts typically facilitate community access because they have recognised leadership qualities and duties; they could represent a church (a minister or lay preacher), school (a principal or teacher), family (the matriarch or patriarch), or territory (the chief or councillor). Even local teachers and heritage workers who collect oral history from a neighbour should choose their contacts judiciously. The goal of this preliminary step seems obvious, but it is frequently discounted. Without knowledge of necessary protocols and possible obstacles, an oral history project grounded in the best academic training could bring more disappointment than success.

Sharpening ideas

Once oral historians consider the possible challenges that await them in fieldwork, the inspiration for their project might be brought into sharper focus. Given the boundless variety of human endeavours, memories and expressions, researchers should attempt to explore a neglected perspective, or a series of unanswered questions, with one proviso: however innovative the topic, an oral historian needs to always remember that even the most compelling ideas have antecedents. Thus, the proposed research should incorporate a survey of relevant bodies of scholarship. Cast the net wide, historian David Henige suggests, for 'without a sure grasp of the literature it will be impossible to proceed to a successful conclusion'. A literature review could involve reading books, articles and encyclopedias; newspapers, magazines and pamphlets; archived reports from missionary organisations and government departments; records in the public domain, such as the telephone directory; and other forms of evidence, such as television and film documentaries. Yet such a broad investigation should not overwhelm project planning. It is advisable to draw up a list of the most useful sources and to catalogue them in a bibliography. The oral historian should take heed, Henige adds, not 'to re-invent the wheel . . . The constant balancing and comparing of sources – challenged or unchallenged, primary or secondary – remains the only way any scholar can hope to achieve a synthesis that will stand the test of time and criticism.'[4]

Using background information, the researcher might draft some open-ended questions that are intended to evoke the fullest responses from an interviewee. To gain a sense of appropriate subjects to discuss, oral historians might construct a questionnaire and hand it out to a focus group of potential interviewees, or consult veteran researchers. Prior to meeting interviewees, it can be helpful for oral historians to memorise simply worded questions that can be posed in a conversational style, as if arising spontaneously.

Thinking logistically

After researchers organise and workshop their ideas, they need to consider the most viable course of action: How many weeks should they spend collecting background information and conducting interviews? What is the envisioned timeframe for transcription? On the one hand, it is wise to narrow the horizon; on the other hand, it is best for researchers to keep an open mind, since short-term goals designed to achieve modest aims can sometimes be extended into an effort that could take several years. Above all, time, budget and the capacity to travel will define the scope of a project. For example, students conducting oral history for a term paper will be constrained by a semester deadline. Many students have limited income, and scant funds could place the hiring of a translator beyond their reach and restrict their field equipment to a basic tape recorder, or even only a pencil and paper. Yet of all logistical issues, transportation – its cost, mode and routes – will rank at the top of the interviewer's principal priorities. In rural South Africa, the relative lack of buses and taxis, as well as their unpredictable schedules, are unavoidable realities. The conditions of roads, especially during bad weather, may also present difficulties. Other pressing considerations include seasonal fog, heat, or cold and rainfall. Additional questions should be asked about the journey, such as: Are there petrol stations and food stores along the way? What provisions should be packed and in what quantity? Will cell phone reception remain strong en route?

Arrival at a research site is no guarantee that organised plans will unfold easily. Before a trip is proposed, the interviewer should anticipate that interviewees (and interpreters, if they are needed) may be out of contact – seeking jobs, teaching school, caring for children, tilling the soil, etc. If participants are ready to talk, there could be other unexplained delays, or additional protocols to follow, which might entail waiting for local authorities to grant access to certain interviewees.[5] Securing clearance and interviewee availability should be one of the first priorities on a basic checklist of pre-interview preparation (see Appendix 1).

Linked to logistics are more intangible concerns relating to the expectations of participants. When first meeting interviewees, the researcher should tell them about the final use of their testimonies and how the research will be returned to them. Indeed, in *Listening for a Change*, Hugo Slim and Paul Thompson urge the interviewer to ' "carry forward" and "give back" something of what he or she has heard' and to make interviewees 'aware of the nature of the transaction which will take place when they tell their story or share their experience'.[6] The oral historian might also ask interviewees what they want to receive, or hope to accomplish, after giving their testimonies. In South African communities struggling with unemployment and poverty, an oral history project might be mistakenly associated with development work, which brings the prospect of jobs and wages. While researchers may present income-earning opportunities if they hire an interpreter, they must be clear about the non-monetary purpose of their fieldwork.

Ethical and legal requirements

The ethical requirements of oral history research in the South African context are discussed more fully in Chapter 3. Like other researchers in the social sciences, oral history practitioners are bound to follow certain norms. Various oral history associations around the world, for example, in the United States and United Kingdom, provide ethical guidelines for their members. In South Africa, the recently established Oral History Association of South Africa (OHASA) has devised a code of conduct for oral history practitioners working in African contexts (see Appendix 2). Globally, these associations propose rigorous rules concerning protocol, copies of release agreements and advice to both interviewers and interviewees, who might be confused by or mistrustful of legal forms. With the release agreement, interviewers face one of their greatest challenges: explaining, in plain terms, the mutual rights of interviewees and oral historians, which encompass 'editing, access restrictions, copyrights, prior use, royalties, and the expected disposition and dissemination of all forms of the record, including the potential for electronic distribution'.[7]

Interviewers are cautioned against making promises to an interviewee that they may not be able to fulfil. In situations where relationships have deepened into ties of trust, the interviewer should adhere to local customs regarding the protection of a person's word. When explained and given at the beginning of a taped interview, verbal consent may be as adequate as written consent, especially for non-literate interviewees. The researcher should also convey to interviewees that they have the right to withdraw from the project; to refuse to discuss any subject; to seal portions of their interview(s); and, most important, to remain anonymous, if they wish.

Official approval may not be needed for more private projects conducted by non-academic researchers who tap into their family networks. Yet even where receiving formal permission is not applicable, it may be necessary to contact an elder in order to conduct an interview. Whatever the case, the researcher's goals and objectives should always be transparent and flexible, particularly if access to a given community or individual is blocked.

Identifying interviewees

Usually, referrals by word of mouth and public records, such as school yearbooks or organisation memberships, enable a researcher to locate interviewees. In more traditional communities, certain gatekeepers, such as preachers, healers, matriarchs and patriarchs, locate and regulate access to interviewees. For a community-based project, a group meeting called by local leaders might point out potential interviewees and help the researcher to note modes of interaction and expression, as well as possible topics of contention. Newspaper, magazine and radio advertisements can also attract potential interviewees. Finally, Internet search engines are increasingly valuable channels for oral historians to find potential participants through online databases containing information that is no longer widely circulated.

Before conducting interviews, it is helpful if researchers can collect a few details about their interviewees. Interviewees with a well-documented public profile may appreciate an interviewer's attention to biographical information. More than flattery, such specific details can shape interview questions and, later, the interpretation of data in the write-up phase.

There are many ways to contact interviewees: by telephone, e-mail, written correspondence and so forth. Interviewees without telephone or mail service might require a letter of invitation or explanation delivered by a community liaison person, or a personal visit by the interviewer. The visit or letter should introduce the researcher and explain the purpose and protocol of his/her project. At this time, it is particularly important to clarify the function of a release document, although this form is generally signed at the time of the interview. Requesting a signature on a document may make the interviewee anxious, suspicious or reluctant to proceed, even when the purpose of the release document is explained. Hence, the researcher should convey the voluntary nature of participation and assure interviewees of their right to withdraw at any time.

When scheduling interviews, the researcher should think carefully about the best location. Here, an awareness of local dynamics and rhythms of labour might determine whether an interviewee's living room, community hall, chief's residence or under a shady tree is a suitable place for a quiet conversation. Wherever they meet, both interviewee and researcher should feel comfortable in a setting with minimal distractions, interruptions and noises. Unless the researcher is known and trusted, it is advisable to err on the side of caution and to recognise that codes of customary respect may entail stringent gender divisions; here, the need for the researcher and interviewee to be the same sex will be an overriding concern.

Using equipment

The logistical considerations discussed in the previous sections of this chapter might give the researcher a better sense of the 'who, what and where' of an oral history project. The 'how' often involves recording and duplicating equipment, and is dependent on the financial resources available. The most basic forms of technology used in the interview process are the tape recorder and paper and pen. Today, digital audio recorders have substantial advantages, such as longer recording time, easy back-up and storage features, and links with software programs that automatically transcribe speech and phonetically spell unrecognised terms. If affordable, a small video camera is probably ideal, as more and more oral historians favouring its use will attest. They realise that visual and audio evidence amplifies the spoken word; they have seen how an interviewee can emphasise a point with a beaming smile, the wink of an eye or a shrug of the shoulders. In these moments of physical communication, a tape recorder or pen may capture only a few words or nothing at all. Furthermore, Donald Ritchie points out that '[audio] recordings convey tone, rhythm, volume, and speech patterns . . . but the facial expressions and body language captured by videotape reveal even more of an interviewee's personality'.[8] Finally, oral historians need to be prepared for an interviewee who does not allow for any recording technology, including pen and paper. In this case, researchers must rely on their memories alone.

Any type of technology should be operated as unobtrusively as possible. Fumbling with a tape recorder can do more to distract an interviewee than the rumble of an impending thunderstorm or any other external distractions. The researcher should also remember to test sound quality in advance and to carry extra tapes and batteries. In addition, interviewees might agree to be recorded, but change their minds midway through an interview, explaining that the tape recorder makes them feel uncomfortable. Thus, a pen and paper should always be handy. Countless oral historians have discovered at the end of an interview, when the tape recorder is already stowed away, that an interviewee seems to unwind and enter a state of relaxation, which allows for fuller or even extraordinary disclosures. In such cases, the interviewer should quickly locate a quiet place and write down the interviewee's admissions.[9]

Scheduling interviews

Technology is important, but patience and people skills are even more important, especially when carrying out interviews. Interviewees are bestowing the gift of their memories. So if difficulties arise in locating interviewees, or if appointments do not begin at a fixed hour, the mantra 'timing and flexibility' is crucial to keep in mind. The oral historian should also be ready for other trials and tribulations, such as a one-on-one interview transforming into a productive, if unwieldy, group discussion or a two-hour afternoon session stretching late into the evening. The historian Philip Bonner reflected on this point in an interview. He described a revelatory moment in a project that sought to document the life stories of aging underworld figures in a black township on the East Rand. One retired male gang leader was identified as a potentially vital source of information, but he stayed away from Bonner, perhaps suspecting that the 'outside researcher would bring the authorities'. Finally, Bonner and the elusive interviewee met, whereupon the latter insisted: 'Now you will sit here until I am finished telling you my story.' At the end of a very long conversation that filled several audiotapes and took the better part of a day, Bonner was ordered to abide by a strict procedure before contacting other gang members and to follow an interview sequence that the interviewee explicitly prescribed.[10]

This situation raises another problem for which there is no firm resolution. Historians such as Henige and Ritchie recommend that an interview last no more than two hours to avoid fatiguing an interviewee. Yet some of their colleagues believe that an elastic conversation over several days is also acceptable practice in certain circumstances – for example, when the researcher is staying for some time in an interviewee's community. By adopting participatory observation techniques developed by anthropologists, as well as periodically recording testimony, the researcher can gather and reconstruct data in a descriptive narrative.

Opening communication

While there is no standard guide that tells researchers how to identify interviewees, there are at least two tried-and-true ways to begin an interview: (1) acknowledge verbally the date and name of the location, and (2) elicit the interviewee's full name, even if it is known already, birth details, marital status and some vital genealogy. Successive questions might subtly investigate the interviewee's social relations, religious faith and so on.[11]

Interviews should be conducted in the interviewee's preferred language.[12] If this is a language other than English, ideally the researcher should be fluent enough to conduct the interview in the chosen language. Since multilingual ability is difficult to achieve for many researchers, they will need to secure the right interpreter, although they should still endeavour to learn introductions and how to make formal requests in the interviewee's language. Some of the most qualified interpreters tend to be teachers, advanced students, or community liaison people working with non-governmental organisations (NGOs). If possible, there should be a back-up interpreter to call in case of an emergency.[13]

The interviewer should be clear from the outset of negotiations with a potential translator regarding the terms of employment, keeping in mind that monetary compensation is usually, if not always, welcomed. Beyond dual-language proficiency, an interpreter needs to be able to recognise non-linguistic cues and to put interviewees at ease. Moreover, an interpreter should have the poise and determination to convey what is appropriate behaviour to the researcher, including hand movements, posture and seating arrangements, which influence the nature of an interview. Just as a translator in an interview might seek to strike a good balance between neutrality and assertion, he/she may also need to interpret an interviewee's words, elaborating on idiomatic meanings in the original spoken testimony.

The most effective research hinges on receptive communication between the interviewer, interpreter, interviewees and other individuals who arrange access to a community of interviewees. Open channels, however, do not imply equal relationships, as the flow of power is uneven. Interpreters appear to control the conversation when they are the main conduit of information. In other instances, oral historians seem to wield authority because they ask the questions. Still, during long phases of an interview, the interviewee alone directs what is said and heard. Ultimately, interviewees exercise extensive influence over the collection of oral history by selecting and reconstructing their memories. For example, when oral historian Nokhaya Makiwane approached *amanyano* groups (African Christian women's organisations) in Sobantu, KwaZulu-Natal, to ask them about the legacies of apartheid rule, her interviewees chose instead to discuss what they called 'private apartheid', the unequal gender relations in their homes that subordinated wives and daughters, preventing them from becoming decision-makers. Makiwane, who thought her interviewees would remain quiet about domestic tensions, allowed this shift in focus to take place.[14] At any time, the interpreter, researcher and interviewee might use silence as a means to relinquish or regain control over a dialogue. Spoken words and their inflections carry imprints of power and pain, which can be understood in terms of rural and urban divisions, class position (employed versus jobless), generational rank, psychological trauma, etc.[15]

Oral historians who spend considerable time with interviewees emphasise the importance of learning the culture of power governing social interactions.[16] The researcher should make every effort to be aware of age and gender protocols that govern hierarchical relationships. For example, if a male interviewer sets up a one-on-one interview with an unaccompanied female interviewee, this meeting could stir unease in a patriarchal community. The presence of an observer, such as the interviewee's husband or older brother, might be required. There are advantages to this arrangement (i.e. cross-checking of information), but there are also serious short-comings, as an observer could become a censor.

While strictly following etiquette is one way of showing familiarity with interviewees, the researcher should not try to be someone they are not. Interviewers who flatter their interviewees needlessly stand out in a conversation. At the same time, researchers should feel comfortable about displaying empathy if the dialogue deals with emotional difficulties that upset the interviewee. Oral historians who work in communities afflicted by widespread civil, domestic or sexual violence, for example, sometimes carry a list of church- or NGO-sponsored counsellors who aid traumatised people.[17]

Propriety entails honouring local standards of politeness when accepting or declining meals. As a gesture of thanks, the interviewer may also want to reciprocate with a gift, such as tea and biscuits. In settings where drinking alcohol is a part of hospitality, the researcher (if he/she is not a minor) may decide to imbibe. However, he/she should drink responsibly, so as not to impair thought and speech. Customary sanctions regulating when alcohol may be consumed should also be adhered to. For example, in some rural Zulu patriarchal homesteads, an interview might only commence after a libation to the ancestors (*amadlozi*), which enables an older male interviewee to recognise his sacred obligation, before recalling his lineage past. Another example is the idea of traditional respect (*ukuhlonipha*) in many rural chiefdoms in KwaZulu-Natal, which could fundamentally alter how a young male interviewer might be expected to behave or how he might be positioned, i.e. on a lower stool in relation to a patriarchal interviewee sitting on a higher chair, or the way in which a topic might be broached with a group of married women who sit on a mat and avoid direct eye contact. Whether researchers like it or not, in some communities *ukuhlonipha* will draw them into their interviewees' world and make them more accountable for recognising taboo subjects, such as sexuality and illness. Similarly, class-based norms influence interview etiquette, subtly dictating allowable topics and the language in which these topics are discussed.

Outsider, insider[18]

Oral historians need to consider their involvement with inter-viewees carefully. To be sure, closer associations can create better understandings, but they can also strain a researcher's professional commitment to critical examination. A professor of Theology at the University of KwaZulu-Natal, Isabel Phiri, found herself in this quandary while studying spiritual healing in evangelical churches led by women in Malawi. Her methodology focused in part on the life story of one charismatic female preacher. Phiri devoted hours every day to attending this preacher's services and joined congregants when they fasted. During one ceremony, when the minister was healing, Phiri felt as if she was 'losing her objectivity'. Phiri recalled the question she posed to herself at that moment: Should she, the academic, step back or move closer? She decided to immerse herself further in the intense milieu. She wanted 'to be part of the church itself so that you write what you see'. Her act of 'seeing' was intended to allow her to gain deeper insight into what her main interviewee hoped to achieve. Phiri's narrative of this experience is quoted at length below:

> On this one occasion, I felt her coming close to me; she touched me. But I also wanted to see what it is that she was doing because she was not only praying for me. I was also doing research. So I opened my eyes just as she was passing me. And at that moment I felt a power that lifted me up in the air and threw me down on the floor. I felt powerless from my head to my toes. I could not even move my hand. I lost total control of my body. But she ignored me . . . When people were going out, she came and picked me up and I went outside.
>
> I was so confused. I didn't understand what had happened at that point . . . [Later] I felt that same power coming back in, but this time I resisted. I decided I wasn't going to fall and I held on to the pillar which was next to me. And I stopped praying, because it was like I am fighting a battle now. I didn't fall in that particular service. And afterwards I wanted to speak to her, to find out what had happened. But she didn't want to speak to me . . . And from there onwards, I didn't have a

chance to speak to her again. I guess . . . I decided to call it a day. I said, this is too much.

. . . A year later I went back, because I wanted to check some facts. And so I told her what I had written, and she was telling me how wrong I was in everything I had written. But, you know, she never gave me a proper interview until I cut the relationship off . . . When I went back the second time, I felt I was more in control because now I knew exactly what I would accept and what I wouldn't accept anymore. The first time I was there I was naïve, so I allowed myself to be drawn in until I lost control. But the second time, when I went there, I went as an interviewer, so I didn't attend any services anymore. I just wanted to have an interview with her. And I made it clear that this time I would not attend services.[19]

Experienced researchers often describe fortunate incidents, such as suddenly coming across an interviewee with free time to talk. The same researchers can also recount trying in vain to elicit vital information from an interviewee. Becoming known in the project area is an excellent way for interviewers to gain access to interviewees, but even the highest degree of insider status, as historian Mxolisi Mchunu explains, has drawbacks. 'It is easier to get into the initial stages, to arrange to talk to people,' he says, but speaking of a particular project, he recalls:

it was more difficult [for the interviewees] to tell me secrets, because unlike an outsider, I will not just leave . . . I found that with confidential things it might have been easier for them to talk to an outsider . . . [It] would be difficult for old men to talk to me because then I would know things about their family. I am from that area, so they might worry that I would talk to others. I think it is better to do interviews in an area where you are not known.[20]

A researcher's insider status might be cause for annoyance if it is not carefully negotiated. In an interview, historian Dingani Mthethwa described an incident that occurred during his investigation of communal land rights in his home region of Maputaland, in northern KwaZulu-Natal. One summer's morning, he was driving on a dirt track and saw an old woman tilling her field. He stopped his car, got out and walked to within hailing distance. Mthethwa respectfully introduced himself in isiZulu; she recognised his surname and familiar isiGonde (a local dialect) inflection. Mthethwa revealed in his greeting that he was not only a neighbour, but also someone who spoke politely to matriarchs in their preferred (Thonga) dialect of isiGonde. They exchanged greetings. As the sun baked and bugs droned, Mthethwa asked her if they could discuss a matter relating to his study of land-use. She replied: 'Only a man, and a young man, would ask me, a toiling grandmother in the heat and insects, raising the crops that feed her children like you, for a little time to talk. Can't you see I am working!?'[21] No formal interview resulted from this conversation.

Processing testimony

With the completion of interviews, the pre-editing phase usually begins, which consists of labelling and transcribing tapes (if an audio/visual recorder is employed), filing the release agreement forms, checking facts and writing up the research. The issue of translation often reflects the purpose of an oral history project. If English-speaking oral historians, for example, required an interpreter to translate the testimony of an isiZulu-speaking interviewee, they could keep two transcripts, one containing the words heard at the interview, the other containing their translation into English, the lingua franca of academia and general audiences in South Africa. Similarly, if isiXhosa-speaking researchers conducted an interview in their own language, or a patois sprinkled with English words, they could elect simply to transcribe the testimony, for they and their intended (community) audiences require no translation.

In the absence of computer-linked transcription technology, manual transcription can be a very laborious process. Even more time-consuming is the translation of a transcribed interview – up to ten hours for each hour of an interview. The lengthiness of these phases must be factored into a project from the start. When transcription and translation are complete, ethical guidelines dictate that printed copies of an interview be delivered to the interviewee for additional fact-checking, i.e. the spelling of names, places, etc. Interviewees may elect to add comments and further amendments, as well as to elide words, sentences and even entire paragraphs. If the researcher has borrowed any supplementary materials, such as photographs, from the interviewees, they should be duplicated (scanned) and returned at this point.

When the project is completed, the labelled tapes, transcripts, videos and any related materials, such as photographs, could be given to an archive or research library, which would make them more broadly accessible.[22] Innovative preservation media will inevitably replace the technology used today to preserve oral history. Thus, researchers and archivists should ensure that original interview transcripts are duplicated and stored at multiple sites. One of the simplest ways to anticipate technological change is to rely on a viable older method. The best immunity to planned obsolescence is a well-preserved and safely stored transcript.

Evaluating the interview material

In the next phase, the researcher focuses on editing: organising evidence and delineating thematic content. The transcribed data might be triangulated, i.e. compared with relevant archival and scholarly sources listed in the bibliographic survey of existing literature. Such cross-checking may corroborate key details, although the subjective nature of some memories may never be fully verifiable. Personal testimony is vulnerable to cultural biases and self-selection, among other factors.[23] More important, perhaps because oral memories are so open to immediate challenge and revision during an interview, personal testimony may be particularly vulnerable to bias and censure. Furthermore, interviewees who describe events that occurred only a day previously may err in their recollection. When they testify about experiences that occurred years or decades in the past, they may have more substantial memory lapses. Thus, noting inaccuracies should not cause undue alarm.

In evaluating the interview material, the researcher needs to consider how different analytical perspectives illuminate complementary and contradictory evidence. Here, the interviewer's insider/outsider status should be reassessed; so too should interviewees' perceptions of racial categories, gender relations, class dynamics, etc. Various scholarly approaches to understanding memory might be incorporated as well. A project that seeks to document how people recall their pasts raises concerns that extend beyond history with a capital 'H'.[24] Thus, where applicable, social sciences, such as psychology, can be used to enhance the investigation.

Giving back

Bringing closure to a project should never be a tangential concern.[25] Although researchers should keep this in mind from the start, near the end of their work they will need to decide on an appropriate way to give back to interviewees. Oral historians with limited funds may only be able to present copies of interview transcripts. Nonetheless, this record may be very meaningful. Nor can one predict the afterlife of the final scholarly product, as historian Peter Delius discovered. He explains: 'I was always careful to bring something back, in terms of the published material. For my research on the Pedi, I brought them a copy of *The Land Belongs to Us*.' This study investigated an African kingdom's struggle to repulse European invaders at the end of the nineteenth century.[26] In the late-apartheid period, black teachers in the former Pedi kingdom, then called Lebowa, in the eastern Transvaal, assigned excerpts of the book in their schools to show students that they were not subjects of white rule, but descendants of anti-colonial resisters. 'The book,' Delius said, 'was [also] used by community members in trying to settle an internal land dispute', which was a cause of tension at his Pedi research site.[27] Another example of giving back is a memory box containing typed transcripts and audiotapes of an interviewee's testimony. A celebratory witness session might also be organised for interviewees and interested community members. At this event, researchers might summarise their findings and invite interviewees to recap briefly their testimonies.[28] Above all, project participants should feel their contributions hold value and will not become the sole property of an interviewer whom they may never see again.

If researchers are uneasy about the broader impact of oral history, they could ask, 'Why should we serve wider audiences beyond academia?' This fair and critical question will doubtless provoke various responses. If interviewers want recorded memories to benefit community development, there is evidence that oral history projects encourage people to express their views of painful events. In fact, oral history in contemporary KwaZulu-Natal is opening channels of healing communication, as Nokhaya Makiwane, a co-ordinator for the Memory Box Programme at the University of KwaZulu-Natal, observed during group interviews in African churches wary of outsiders. Makiwane recalled: 'One of [the women] reprimanded the others, "How can you speak of such things in front of strangers?" Another woman replied, "We never had the opportunity to speak of these things before. It's like we're bonding even more now . . . We have a chance to talk about challenges in our families, in our lives." ' Makiwane continued to hold these conversations, eventually fostering 'a sense of community that spread to other parts of their lives . . . [and their] family members'. The interviews, Makiwane concluded, brought the women 'together as a team', which gave 'them some skill as well, to co-ordinate, to make things happen'.[29]

Thus, oral history advances basic goals of development encapsulated in participatory rural appraisal (PRA) projects that seek to alleviate poverty by augmenting local resources from human capital to material resources. Similar to oral history, the objectives of PRA recognise people within a community as agents of change, who are capable of speaking for themselves.[30] Some oral historians and development workers share a similar outlook and they are invested in what tomorrow might bring. As historians Roy Rosenzweig and David Thelen discovered in *The Presence of the Past*, their interviewees regarded the past as meaningful because of 'the futures they wanted to carve for themselves'.[31] With this in mind, interviewers entering the field should know that they too are part of a mutually created future – in fact, a potentially exciting future where fieldwork challenges need not stand in the way of bringing the past to life. Researchers who are willing to be flexible, patient and open may enjoy the rich benefits that come with learning more about others – and themselves – in an oral history project.

Notes

1. We dedicate this chapter to the late Roy Rosenzweig, pioneering oral historian, colleague and friend. Our title is taken from Donald Ritchie, *Doing Oral History* (New York: Twayne Publishers, 1995).
2. The oral historian could consider a number of approaches, such as life stories or single-issue interviewing. The life-story method seeks to examine the full arc of one individual's existence; see Barbara Sommer and Mary Kay Quinlan, *Oral History Manual* (New York: Alta Mira Press, 2002). In contrast, the single-issue method concentrates on a major area of personal expertise, such as the practice of traditional medicine, or an individual's experiences during a singular episode (i.e. an environmental crisis like a drought, or political protest).
3. We are using the term 'researchers' broadly, to designate anyone who is conducting an oral history project, including individuals who are themselves members of the group under study. This may include teachers, students, community activists and others.
4. David Henige, *Oral Historiography* (London: Longman, 1982), 25.
5. Interview protocol will obviously vary according to local dynamics. In areas where African customary law prevails, an audience with traditional authorities, who exercise rights to grant or deny access to a person or community, will be crucial before interviewees are identified and approached. For further details, see Chapters 5 and 6.
6. Hugo Slim and Paul Thompson, *Listening for a Change: Oral Testimony and Community Development* (London: Panos Publications, 1993), 153.

7. Ibid. See also Chapter 3 of this volume; Oral History Association (OHA), 'Oral History Evaluation Guidelines, Pamphlet No. 3', 21. http://www.dickinson.edu/organizations/oha/pub_eg.html, accessed 21 June 2006.

8. Ritchie, *Doing Oral History*, 109.

9. Some release documents may permit the use of pre- and post-interview testimony.

10. Interview, Benedict Carton and Louise Vis with Philip Bonner, 7 July 2005, Johannesburg. For scholarship that emerged from Bonner's interviews, see Philip Bonner, 'The Russians on the Reef, 1947–57: Urbanisation, Gang Warfare and Ethnic Mobilisation', in *Apartheid's Genesis, 1935–1962*, ed. Philip Bonner, Peter Delius and Deborah Posel (Johannesburg: Witwatersrand University Press, 1993), 160–94.

11. In this section, we follow the suggestions of Slim and Thompson, *Listening for a Change*, 64–65.

12. For example, an interviewee whose mother tongue is isiZulu may choose to speak in English to an English-speaking researcher in order to be polite or to establish his/her standing as an educated person. However, as Radikobo Ntsimane makes clear in Chapter 5, interviewees are the ultimate owners of their stories, which they might choose to convey in their preferred language.

13. For more on interpreters, see Chapter 5.

14. For an analysis of some of these interviews, see Philippe Denis, ' "We Also Had to Live with Apartheid in Our Homes": Stories of Women in Sobantu, South Africa', *Studia Historiae Ecclesiasticae* 30, no. 1 (June 2004): 151–67. These interviews were conducted in 2000 and 2001. Most of the female interviewees requested anonymity.

15. On the subtexts of pain and trauma in oral history interviews, see Chapter 7.

16. Radikobo Ntsimane explores cultural dynamics in Chapter 5 and covers the central issues raised in this section. Philippe Denis explains the importance of learning the interviewee's culture as an ethical requirement of oral history in Chapter 3.

17. For example, oral historians could make up a list of the most accessible free or sliding-scale community-based counselling services in the area in which they are conducting their interviews.

18. See Chapter 5 for a fuller discussion of outsider-insider divisions.

19. Interview, Louise Vis with Professor Isabel Phiri, April 2004, Pietermaritzburg.

20. Interview, Benedict Carton and Louise Vis with Mxolisi Mchunu, 9 July 2004, Durban. The interviews Mchunu conducted provided key data for his groundbreaking study 'Discipline, Respect and Ethnicity: A Study of the Changing Patterns of Fatherhood of Three Generations of Zulu Fathers and Sons in KwaShange, Inadi, Vulindlela Area of Pietermaritzburg, KwaZulu-Natal, from the 1930s to the 1990s' (Master's thesis, University of KwaZulu-Natal, Durban, 2005).

21. Interview, Benedict Carton with Dingani Mthethwa, 21 September 2003, Washington, DC. Mthethwa also stated that an interviewee might give more (and different) information to 'outside researchers on the assumption that they do not have deep knowledge of community dynamics'. For example, a foreign-born, visiting oral historian in South Africa may hear a fuller 'account of how apartheid rule invaded everyday life because the interviewee assumes that the researcher is not familiar' with the daily injustices of the former racial order. Mthethwa's Maputaland interviews were used in his book chapter 'Two Bulls in One Kraal: Local Politics, "Zulu History", and Heritage Tourism in Kosi Bay, KwaZulu-Natal', in *Zulu Identities: Being Zulu, Past and Present*, ed. Benedict Carton, John Laband and Jabulani Sithole (Pietermaritzburg: University of KwaZulu-Natal Press; London: Christopher Hurst; New York: Columbia University Press, 2008).

22. The following basic information should be placed on a label: the interviewee's name, the interviewer's name, the date and the location of the interview.

23. Norman Denzin and Yvonna Lincoln, eds., *Handbook of Qualitative Research* (Thousand Oaks, CA: Sage, 2000).

24. For a critical scholarly discussion of the changing methodologies shaping South African history with a capital 'H' in the post-apartheid era, see Tim Nuttall and John Wright, 'Exploring beyond History with a Capital "H"', *Current Writing* 10, no. 2 (1998): 38–61.

25. For a more comprehensive discussion of the importance of giving back to interviewees, see Chapter 3.

26. Peter Delius, *The Land Belongs to Us: The Pedi Polity, the Boers and the British in the Nineteenth-Century Transvaal* (Johannesburg: Ravan Press, 1983).

27. Interview, Benedict Carton and Louise Vis with Peter Delius, 7 July 2005, Johannesburg.

28. Witness sessions have their drawbacks. In such a public forum, community leaders may put pressure on interviewees to sanction a consensus account. Moreover, there may be discrepancies in testimony, which could provoke acrimony and recrimination.

29. Interview, Louise Vis with Nokhaya Makiwane, February 2004, Pietermaritzburg. In other instances, conducting interviews in a community divided by age-based hierarchies has prompted community members to reach out in a spirit of greater social inclusion, 'closing the gap between generations' to 'revitalis[e] those marginalised by age or any other "disadvantages"': Slim and Thompson, *Listening for a Change*, 15.

30. Slim and Thompson, *Listening for a Change*, 56–57.

31. Roy Rosenzweig and David Thelen, *The Presence of the Past: Popular Uses of History in American Life* (New York: Columbia University Press, 1998), 37.

3

The Ethics of Oral History

PHILIPPE DENIS

THE PURPOSE OF this chapter is to help oral history practitioners to reflect on the ethics of their discipline. The main aim of research ethics is to protect the welfare of the research participants.[1] Following an international trend, social science research institutions in South Africa now require all researchers to adhere to strictly defined ethical guidelines. The *Health Act 61 of 2003* stipulates that an independent accredited research ethics committee must approve all research involving human participants.[2] In theory, this applies to oral history, although the manner in which the legislation will be put into practice in this field of research remains unclear. It is in the biomedical field, where the risk of harm to research participants is the highest, that for the first time – after the trial of several Nazi doctors in 1948 in Nuremberg – the need was felt to regulate the ethical behaviour of researchers. However, social science research also carries risks, although often on a lesser and qualitatively different scale. Until the closing decades of the twentieth century, the general rule for the humanities in most universities and research institutions was that the ethical conduct of research was a matter for the conscience of the individual researcher and for informal policing by the broader research community.[3] However, this is changing and, even in history, there is a growing recognition of the need to regulate researchers' use of private documents, which may harm the reputation of the people investigated or their descendants.[4]

Nobody disputes the fact that oral history practitioners are bound to follow certain ethical norms. Various oral history associations around the world, in the United States[5] and in the United Kingdom,[6] for instance, provide ethical guidelines for their members. In South Africa some work has been done, notably by the newly established Oral History Association of South Africa (OHASA), on a code of conduct for oral history practitioners working in an African context (see Appendix 2). In recent years, a debate has taken place about the ethics of biomedical research in developing countries. 'Benchmarks of ethical research', such as those proposed by Ezekiel Emanuel and his colleagues from the National Institutes of Health of Bethesda, Maryland,[7] are now widely used in the research community. A similar reflection is needed for oral history in view, among other things, of the rights of the indigenous communities involved in oral history projects.

This chapter primarily deals with the ethics of oral history in South Africa: the moral obligations that a practitioner has in conducting an oral history project. There are various ways of determining what is right and wrong in a given situation and I shall not discuss them here. Suffice to say that certain oral history projects may not only cause harm – for instance, when an offensive statement causes conflict in the group concerned – but may also be morally wrong, as in the case of a reprehensible act done without the knowledge of those who may suffer from its outcomes, such as the voluntary distortion of an uneducated person's point of view in an academic publication.[8]

Of less immediate concern to oral history practitioners is whether their enterprises conform to the laws of the country in which they are working. Being ethical and being legal are two different matters. Even in a highly litigious country such as the United States, oral history is not a fertile area for lawsuits.[9] In South Africa the probability of a legal action against an oral historian is even slimmer. This is because the types of legal injury for which oral historians may be held accountable are not extensive. I shall deal here with some of these legal issues, especially in the section dealing with copyright, but the emphasis will be on ethical requirements.

Oral history, social science and journalism

It is important to distinguish between oral history and other forms of social practices involving interviews, as this will help to clarify the specificity of oral history in matters of research ethics. Two cognate disciplines also rely on interviews, but in a different way and with different ethical requirements. Social scientists, such as sociologists and clinical psychologists, routinely conduct interviews, either on a one-on-one basis or by way of focus groups. The purpose of these interviews is to gather knowledge on the individuals or groups involved in the research. Once the research is over, the material collected by the researchers is discarded. Unless otherwise agreed, any kind of personal information remains absolutely confidential. A model of a consent form in use at the University of the Witwatersrand thus stipulates that the recordings 'will be kept securely in a locked environment and will be destroyed or erased once data capture and analysis are complete'.[10] Due to the nature of their discipline, oral history practitioners do exactly the opposite. For them the main purpose of an interview is to collect oral information for future use. The identity of the informants is made public if they sign a release form to that effect. The preservation and dissemination of the interviews are an essential aspect of oral history. An oral historian always doubles as an archivist.

Another category of professionals regularly involved in interviews is journalists. Unlike oral history practitioners, journalists rarely retain their notes or their audiotapes for posterity. Their objective is immediate: it is the writing of an article that will be published the following day, week, or month. They are usually driven by very strict deadlines. This does not mean that journalism has no ethical guidelines, but these are different from those of social scientists or historians. Journalists tend to take notes, rather than tape-record their interviews, and generally use only brief excerpts from interviews in their stories. They do not need formal release agreements. The assumption is that people who respond to journalists' questions know that their words will appear in print, unless they stipulate that something is off the record, or otherwise not for attribution.[11]

Oral history and ethics review committees

While research ethics committees (RECs) are well established in faculties of medicine and health science research institutions in South Africa, they are only starting to develop in faculties of humanities and social science research. Ethical review is increasingly becoming mandatory for social science research involving human participants. At the same time, the concept remains controversial.[12] Opponents argue that most ethics committee members, in South Africa at least, are poorly trained or unacquainted with the methods of qualitative research and that the bureaucratic procedures imposed on researchers cause unnecessary delays. Proponents of RECs, on the other hand, stress that an ethical review, if competently conducted, can add value to the proposed study and may alert researchers to various forms of harm they have not considered. An independent assessment helps to determine risks.

How does this apply to oral history? It is worth noting that in the United States, a country where ethical review has long been mandatory in social science and is now practised almost universally, the Office for Human Research Protection in the Department of Health and Human Services issued a clarification in 2003, according to which most oral history should not be considered research under the purview of institutional review boards (IRBs – the American equivalent of RECs). This policy clarification, however, was largely ignored by most universities' IRBs, as highlighted on different occasions in *Perspectives*, the American Historical Association's newsletter.[13] At a conference called 'Human Subject Regulation and Research outside the Biomedical Sphere' in April 2003, a multidisciplinary group of scholars convened by the Center for Advanced Study of the University of Illinois unambiguously recommended that oral history should be removed altogether from IRB review:

> We recommend focusing on those areas of research that pose the greatest risk, such as biomedical research, while removing or reducing scrutiny of many fields within the social sciences and humanities that pose minimal risk. Some fields, such as journalism and ethnography, and methods, such as oral history, have their own, well-established sets of ethical guidelines and appeal procedures. In addition, they pose virtually no risk to the subjects.[14]

In South Africa, both in oral history, as an established academic discipline, and in the social sciences, ethical reviews are relatively new. The need for a code of conduct for oral history practitioners is self-evident, but if the community of oral historians agrees to regulate itself, under the auspices of OHASA or a similar professional group, there might be grounds, just as in the United States, for exempting oral history from formal ethical review.

Basic ethical principles

The literature on research ethics commonly distinguishes between the philosophical principles guiding ethical research and the ethical guidelines or benchmarks that apply these principles. Before examining the practice of oral history, I shall briefly review four of these principles, which all have a direct bearing on oral history and are widely accepted in research ethics.[15]

Autonomy and respect for people's dignity

The first philosophical principle is recognising autonomy and respecting the dignity of the person or group of people who are interviewed. It is a concern for their dignity that motivates the practice of seeking their informed consent and offering them guarantees of confidentiality. This principle is particularly relevant when one deals with the people whom, for want of a better word, I shall call indigenous. An increasing number of oral history projects in South Africa focus on the lives and histories of people who identify themselves in this way. The rights of these people, which have been so often ignored in the past, should be respected by all the researchers who record their stories. The principles of autonomy and respect for the dignity of the person is the foundation of the three principles highlighted by Erica-Irene Daes in her opening address to the World Intellectual Property Organisation (WIPO) round table on intellectual property and indigenous peoples in 1998 in Geneva:

1. Indigenous peoples should be recognised as the primary guardians and interpreters of their cultures, arts and sciences, whether created in the past, or developed by them in the future.
2. Indigenous peoples are recognised as collective legal owners of their knowledge, in perpetuity.
3. The right to learn and use indigenous knowledge can be acquired only in accordance with the laws or customary procedures of the indigenous peoples concerned, and with their free and informed consent.[16]

When conducting an oral history project in a local community – for example, a tribal area in South Africa – oral history practitioners should always keep in mind that the ownership of the stories that they collect will always be contested. The implication is that they should respect the limitations imposed by the interviewees for the use of their stories. For all their expertise, academics involved in this kind of research may not claim exclusive control over the oral history process. They have an obligation to involve the people concerned in the research design. From an indigenous perspective, the oral traditions of the communities concerned are sacred; some remain secret. Traditional leaders have a responsibility to ensure that the sacred character of ancestral traditions is always respected.[17]

Non-maleficence

It is the oral history practitioner's responsibility to ensure that any harm resulting from the interview process is kept to an absolute minimum. Any researcher has a moral obligation to consider the possibility of harm as a direct or indirect consequence of his/her research. There are several ways, as shall be seen later, in which an interview may cause what the United Kingdom's *Freedom of Information Act of 2000* describes as 'distress'.[18] The harm may result from the interview itself, or from unintended consequences of the dissemination of interview material. In a disadvantaged community, raising false expectations when requesting permission to conduct an interview is a common and particularly problematic way of causing harm to an interviewee. Insensitivity to the interviewee's emotional responses to distressing content is another common form of harm that researchers should be aware of and do their utmost to avoid.

Beneficence

From an ethical point of view, the most crucial duty for an oral history practitioner is to minimise the risk of harm when an interview is conducted, but this is not enough. Programme directors and postgraduate students involved in oral history projects have to ensure that the people they interview also benefit from the interview process. It would not be right that those who conduct the project are the only ones who benefit from the research, be it for their intellectual satisfaction or for the advancement of their academic careers. How the interviewees will benefit from the interview is not always easy to determine, particularly when they live in poverty; this question will be discussed in a later section of this chapter. What the principle of beneficence means is that the oral history practitioner has the duty to explore, preferably in consultation with the person or the group concerned, how they will benefit from the research. It should be noted that payment for interviews does not constitute an appropriate benefit, but compensation should be given for travel or other actual costs to the interviewee.

Justice

Justice, the fourth fundamental ethical principle, requires that people receive what is due to them. In oral history, justice requires that the interviewers treat the interviewees with fairness and equity during all stages of the interview process. This means, for example, that oral history practitioners have a duty to provide care and support to the people they interview should they become distressed or harmed as a result of the interview. Justice also requires that those who stand to benefit from the research should bear the burdens of the research. In most social science research, the burdens of the research are born by the participants, while the benefits accrue to the researcher who gains degrees, publications, prestige and promotions.[19] The people who agree to share their stories and their communities deserve, if the principle of justice is to be observed, some form of reward in the form of a material benefit to the group, or even simply the fact of being affirmed and recognised.

The issue of justice is of particular relevance in traditional communities. When social scientists or oral historians approach community members for an interview, the balance of power usually weighs in their favour. Their expertise, social skills and financial means put them at an advantage and the onus is on them to ensure that they do not abuse their position of power. In the case of heterogeneous communities or communities divided by conflict, it is the researcher's responsibility to take into account the complexities of these social groups. In South Africa, there is a great need to develop ethical awareness about these issues, as existing mechanisms are insufficient for the protection of indigenous people's intellectual and cultural property rights.[20]

Ethical guidelines

The practical implications of the principles of autonomy, non-maleficence, beneficence and justice vary according to the field of research. In oral history, they primarily apply to the relationship between the interviewer and the interviewee and each stage of the interview process has specific ethical requirements.[21]

Planning an oral history project

The first duty of a research manager, a postgraduate student or a schoolteacher who envisages conducting interviews in a given area is to ensure that the benefit that will accrue to the interviewees outweighs the risks they may incur as a result of the interviews. In other words, the decision to go ahead with an oral history project should only be made if the project is thought to present a favourable risk-benefit ratio. In practice, the researcher should have a response to the following questions:

1. What is the purpose of the research project? What is the possible range of future uses to which it might be put?
2. Does the research entail any risks for the participants? If so, can these risks be minimised, or should the research project be modified or abandoned altogether?
3. How should the interviewee be informed of the risks he or she might incur, and how should this be reflected in the release agreement form?

Another requirement is that the research should be scientifically valid. It would be unethical to waste the time and goodwill of community members for a research project that is badly designed. An oral history practitioner needs to acquire sufficient technical knowledge to conduct an interview of the best possible standard. In the case of oral history projects involving fieldworkers, the project managers should select competent interviewers and give them sufficient guidance. They should also ensure that the recordings are processed and preserved in a professional manner.

Oral history practitioners are required to obtain the best possible knowledge about the culture of the people they will interview, particularly if they belong to traditional communities. Ignoring or misrepresenting the interviewees' cultural habits increases the risk of damage to their integrity and self-esteem. The 'Guidelines for the Provision of Psychological Services and for the Conduct of

Psychological Research with Aborigines and Torres Strait Islander People of Australia' are of interest to this discussion, as they apply *mutatis mutandis* to oral history in South Africa:

> It is essential to have knowledge of: the original, indigenous cultures of Australia, the psychological functioning and personal psychological needs of people from those cultures; the cultural and other milieu factors that underlie those needs and ways of applying that knowledge in psychological research with and psychological services for indigenous people. Consequently, psychologists who are likely to be involved in such research or service provision have a professional responsibility to obtain such knowledge.[22]

Before the interview

Once the interview schedule is decided upon, oral historians need to approach the people they would like to interview. From an ethical point of view, this is a critical moment. The exchanges taking place before the interview may determine the quality of the entire interview process. The principle of respect for the autonomy and dignity of persons finds expression in the requirement of informed consent by research participants. The two standard components of consent are the provision of information and ensuring the participants' competence and understanding.

First, the interviewers must inform the people they hope to interview of the purpose of the interview and what is required from them if they agree to be interviewed. They should give background information on the research project. The time and place of the interview need to be clarified, as well as the reasons for recording the conversation on a tape recorder. The interviewees must be informed of their right to refuse the interview, or to withdraw from it at any time, should they wish to do so. The interviewees also have to understand the potential uses to which the material might be put and the extent to which confidentiality will be maintained. It is the interviewer's responsibility to verify that the interviewees fully understand the purpose of the interview, the way in which it will be conducted and its future use. When the interviewers and the interviewees do not share the same cultural background, as is often the case in South Africa, special caution is needed to avoid misunderstandings.

Explicitly or not, some interviewees expect confidentiality and this is an essential part of the negotiation between the interviewer and the interviewee prior to the signing of the consent form or release agreement. When the information is of a confidential nature, or when the interviewees insist that their testimonies, or part of them, should remain confidential, various solutions can be found, such as restricting access to the interview material during a certain period, or using and reporting it anonymously.

Second, once interviewees fully understand the nature and the implications of the oral history project, the interviewer must ensure that they give informed and voluntary consent. Some interviewees give the impression of agreeing to be interviewed because they do not feel free to say no, but at a later stage they express their uneasiness and sometimes object to being interviewed, a situation which raises serious ethical concerns. In the West, an interview has become a common form of enquiry and communication. The large majority of individuals who are interviewed by oral historians know what to expect.[23] This is not necessarily the case in South Africa. Oral history practitioners should never assume that the people they approach are cognisant of their rights and obligations as interviewees.

Whether or not the agreement between the interviewer and the interviewee should be formalised in writing at all times is a matter of debate. As the British oral historian Paul Thompson notes in the third edition of his classic *The Voice of the Past*, a licence to quote the interviewee is implied by the consent to be interviewed. Interviewees who agree to be interviewed, knowing that a historian is collecting material for a research study, would appear to have little legal grounds for complaint if they found themselves quoted in print. In effect, despite their intrinsic limitations, informal understandings have been considered as sufficient for the writing of innumerable sociological and historical studies. An insistence on a formal transfer of legal rights through explicit, written consent may not only worry an informant, but could actually reduce proper protection against exploitation.[24] The *Institutional Review Board Member Handbook* in the United States makes the point that signed consent is not necessary if the risks of harm are very low and if the signed consent form constitutes a potential breach of confidentiality.[25] In vulnerable communities with high levels of suspicion, as is the case with many communities in South Africa, a signed consent form can be perceived as a threat. In these communities, some people have a low level of literacy and a written document – even if it is in their home language – may intimidate them and even dissuade them from participating in a project. For this reason, it may sometimes be more appropriate not to use a written consent form. If the risk of harm is very low, a recorded verbal statement may be sufficient.

However, when interviews are destined to be archived and made accessible to other researchers, as happens with most oral history projects, the use of formal agreements appears to be almost universal.[26] Any works that are published, broadcast, performed or transmitted electronically are covered by copyright legislation; this applies equally to oral history collections. All recordings, according to the South African *Copyright Act 98 of 1978*, are subject to copyright protection.[27]

Copyright law aims to protect products of the intellect from unauthorised usage. By law, the ownership and the operations of a work embodying intellectual content are subject to contract. The copyright of an interview is usually transferred by means of a release agreement, which recognises the joint authorship of the interviewer and the interviewee. The former is the author of the recording as a recording and the latter of the information contained in the recording. A release agreement is a legal document and should be carefully worded. It carries more weight than a simple consent form, which only aims to protect the rights of an informant in a research project. In South Africa, the copyright in an interview remains in force for 50 years after the end of the year in which the interviewee dies. When it expires, the work falls into the public domain and may be freely used by anyone.

The difference between an interview and other forms of intellectual work, such as a book, a song or a poem, is that under normal circumstances its author cannot expect payment for it. An interview with Nelson Mandela, for example, may have a commercial value, but this is an exception. Because they do not expect payment, most interviewees are willing to transfer the copyright of their interviews to sound archives, museums or libraries without monetary compensation. The advantage of such a transfer is that it can prevent the abuse and unauthorised copying of interview material and provide suitable facilities for proper use.[28]

Only complete interviews or substantial parts of interviews are eligible for copyright protection. It is recognised that short extracts of interviews may be used for reviews or research, including theses, without any formal agreement. The doctrine of fair use authorises the use of copyrighted works for enterprises such as criticism, comment, news reporting, teaching, scholarship and research. The use of a relatively small section of an interview is considered to be within the limits of fair use.[29] The South African *Copyright Act 98 of 1978* refers to this doctrine when it says that the copyright of a literary or musical work shall not be infringed by any quotation of these works 'provided that the quotation shall be compatible with fair practice'.[30]

During the interview

When conducting an interview, oral history practitioners should always keep in mind the principle of autonomy and respect for the dignity of persons. Asking people questions about their lives and their actions can be very intrusive. The interviewee may benefit from the exercise in the end, but only if the interview is conducted with sensitivity and empathy. In a diverse country such as South Africa, cultural issues are of paramount importance. Ignoring the cultural background of an interviewee may not only result in a bad interview or no interview at all, but in doing harm.

The need to adopt indigenous styles of interaction when communicating with indigenous people is recognised in other countries around the world, as shown by the 'Guidelines for the Provision of Psychological Services and for the Conduct of Psychological Research with Aborigines and Torres Strait Islander People of Australia', to which reference was made earlier. When conducting an interview with an indigenous person, the document suggests, professionals should be aware of the following factors that may affect the outcome of the encounter:

- the use of appropriate nomenclatures for reference to people of indigenous and non-indigenous descent;
- appropriate forms of greeting and leave-taking;
- gender differences in interpersonal communication, particularly as they affect communication with people of the other gender;
- the cultural use of questioning as a method of information acquisition;
- respectful behaviour, particularly as it affects intergenerational communication;
- the importance of elders and land custodians;
- the use of personal names, including taboos associated with their use;
- non-verbal communication styles, including eye contact or non-contact, ways of expressing emotion, and posture; and
- public displays or other behaviours that are likely to result in feelings of embarrassment and shame.[31]

Another way of showing respect for the interviewee is to acknowledge in an appropriate manner the pain, hurt and emotions that may occur during an interview. A negative reaction, caused by an interviewer's insecurity, can damage an interviewee's self-esteem and, in the worst case, reinforce the trauma. Inexperienced oral history practitioners dread the moment when the person they interview starts to cry. There are various useful techniques, such as attentive listening, sensitive questioning and empathic imagination, which can help the interviewer to contain difficult emotions and create the conditions for healing.[32]

The golden rule when conducting an interview that takes an unexpected turn, either by eliciting strong feelings of pain and sadness or by causing embarrassment and shame, is to give the interviewee the option to withdraw. The informed consent granted by the interviewee before the interview does not give all rights to the interviewer. Oral history practitioners have to verify at each stage of the interview process that the interviewees continue to give their full and uninhibited consent. When they show signs of distress as a result of the interview, the onus is on the interviewer to seek professional advice to alleviate the pain caused by the remembering of difficult memories in the interviewees' lives.

Processing the interview

Science and ethics are not in conflict, as Emanuel and his colleagues argue: valid science is an ethical requirement. Unless research generates reliable and valid data that can be interpreted and used by the specified beneficiaries of the research, it will have no social value and participants will be exposed to risks for no benefit.[33] Oral history practitioners have to ensure that their interviews are documented, indexed, catalogued and made available, as agreed with the interviewees, and that a copy of the recordings or transcripts is transmitted to them.[34] This is easier said than done. In the case of a small oral history project, such as a postgraduate dissertation or a local oral history project, it is the same person who conducts the interviews, labels the tapes, transcribes them, catalogues them and stores them, as well as the transcripts, in a safe place. In the case of larger oral history projects, these various tasks are assigned to different people, under the responsibility of a project manager. In both cases, it can happen that the project is never concluded. Interviews are conducted, but not processed. This is cause for ethical concern. Oral history practitioners have a double responsibility: towards the people they have interviewed and towards the academic community. When they let tapes gather dust in a cupboard, the interviewees who expect feedback from them suffer a prejudice and the community at large also experiences a loss, by being deprived of information about the past that should have been made available. For the same reasons, oral history practitioners have a responsibility to inform the interviewees, preferably in writing, of any change regarding the preservation or dissemination of the interviews. The interviewees should always know where to locate the transcripts and tapes of interviews in which they have participated.

Are oral historians bound to transcribe the entirety of the interviews they have conducted, or have commissioned fieldworkers to conduct for them? If the main goal of the project is the dissemination of information, the answer is yes. Some oral historians, however, do not transcribe interviews because of the cost, or because transcription can blind researchers to aural clues. In a still distant future, new digital technologies may also render transcriptions redundant. In any event, it is recommended not to transcribe and preserve interviews or parts of them when they contain defamatory statements. Where a statement is believed to be false or damaging to the reputation or privacy of a third party, the portion of the interview and the transcript containing the statement should not be made available to researchers and certainly should not be published until the subject of the statement is dead.[35] Where the truth of statements is less clear, the risks and benefits of making the relevant portion of the interview available should be assessed.[36] In some cases, interviews containing libellous or confidential information can be made available if the sources remain anonymous.

What should be done if an interviewee confesses to a serious crime during an interview? The process of recounting one's life often weakens the natural barriers that many people have in place regarding their private lives. Are oral history practitioners obliged to divulge their sources? They are, but only if subpoenaed to make such disclosures in court. They have no obligation to disclose information if no investigation is in progress. However, if they feel a strong moral duty to inform law enforcement officials of a serious crime that the interviewee has admitted to on tape, there is certainly no privileged relationship such as the one between doctors and their patients, or lawyers and their clients, which would prevent them from doing so. The situation is different if the police obtain a court order obliging the interviewers to disclose the contents of the interviews, thus overriding confidentiality agreements made with interviewees. Deliberately evading questioning by police or being evasive or untruthful when questioned may result in conviction for obstructing the course of justice. Courts may similarly require interviewers to give evidence based on the content of interviews.[37] In practice, this is unlikely to happen often since a transcript or tape of an oral history interview is usually considered hearsay in the eyes of the law.

On completion of the project

As mentioned earlier, the principle of beneficence implies that an oral history practitioner has a duty to explore, preferably in consultation with the person or the community concerned, how they will benefit from the project. This is one of the thorniest issues in oral history practice, especially when dealing with poor communities, as is often the case in South Africa. It is not rare to hear oral history practitioners reporting cases of interviewees who expected monetary compensation for their stories. As a general rule, money may only be given to research participants as reimbursement for material costs. For certain research projects, particularly in the biomedical field, some forms of payment, usually small amounts of money, may be necessary to prompt a sufficient number of people to volunteer to serve as research subjects, provided that everything is done to ensure that such payments do not impair the judgement of the research participants.[38] However, in oral history, the practice of making payments to interviewees raises serious difficulties. The first concerns the validity of the information provided. What if the interviewees add juicy details to their life stories in order to increase their remuneration? Another objection is that the exchange of money perverts the relationship between the interviewer and the interviewee. An interview is a human encounter between one person who talks and another who listens. The best benefit someone can receive for telling a story is to know that this story will be treasured by the person who heard it. Telling one's story is often an affirming experience. It helps to develop one's sense of identity and self-esteem. In some cases, it can have a therapeutic effect. On the other hand, it may be acceptable in some contexts to present the interviewee with a gift such as a chicken, a blanket or a bottle of whisky, especially if the interviewee is a person of standing in a traditional community. Of course, when interviewees have a right to royalty fee, as for a broadcast or a biographical collection, this should be secured for them.[39] As pointed out earlier, this is unlikely to happen in South Africa. Oral history practitioners have to ensure that no undue expectations are raised in this respect.

In the end, the interviewees' most important right is to receive feedback on the oral history project in which they participated. At the very least, they should receive a copy of the transcript of their interview, if possible with the tape recording. A public celebration could be held to honour the interviewees and their memories. Going back to the interviewees once the project is completed signals that they remain the co-authors of their interviews. It reaffirms symbolically that they are the owners of their stories, however important the work accomplished by the oral history practitioners may have been.

One should not underestimate the logistical difficulties of this enterprise. Many oral history projects have a limited time span and a tight budget. Often, once the last interview is conducted and transcribed, no time is left to end the project properly by paying a last visit to the interviewees and handing over to them the text of their interviews. To avoid this difficulty, it is crucial to plan the last phase of the project carefully in advance.[40]

Conclusion

Like any other discipline, oral history needs ethical guidelines to reduce the risk of harm to research participants in an interview situation. This applies particularly in South Africa, where interviewers and interviewees can easily be trapped in unequal relationships. It would be unethical, for example, to interview people without informing them of the purpose of the interview. Denying the interviewees the right to withdraw from the interview or being insensitive to their cultural background or their emotional status is also problematic. Oral history practitioners – whether individual researchers using oral history as one technique among others, fieldworkers formally employed in an oral history project, or schoolchildren collecting stories under the supervision of a teacher – should see ethical guidelines not as an obstacle to their freedom of research, but as a way of doing oral history in a professional manner. If the community of oral historians in South Africa agrees to regulate itself, there might be grounds, as in other countries, for exempting oral history from formal ethical review.

Notes

1. Douglas Wassenaar, 'Ethical Issues in Social Science Research', in *Research in Practice: Applied Methods for the Social Sciences*, ed. Martin Terreblanche, Kevin Durrheim and Desmond Painter (Cape Town: University of Cape Town Press, 2006), 60–79. I owe a special debt to Douglas Wassenaar, my colleague at the University of KwaZulu-Natal, for his insightful comments.
2. *Health Act 61 of 2003*, Chapter 9, section 71.
3. See Robert Cribb, 'Ethical Regulation and Humanities in Australia: Problems and Consequences', *Monash Bioethics Review* 23, no. 3 (2004): 39–57.
4. For a South African example, see Julie Parle, 'The Voice of History? Archives, Ethics and Historians', *Journal of Natal and Zulu History* 24–25 (2006–2007): 164–87.

5. See 'Principles and Standards of the Oral History Association', an appendix in *Oral History and the Law*, 3rd ed., John A. Neuenschwander (Carlisle, Pennsylvania: Oral History Association, 2002), 65–68.

6. Alan Ward, 'Oral History Society Ethical Guidelines', in *Is Your Oral History Legal and Ethical?* http://www.oralhistory.org.uk/ethics, accessed 10 May 2008.

7. Ezekiel Emanuel, David Wendler, Jack Killen and Christine Grady, 'What Makes Clinical Research in Developing Countries Ethical? The Benchmark of Ethical Research', *Journal of Infectious Diseases* 189 (2004): 930–37.

8. This brief reflection on ethics is based on William David Ross's moral theory; in particular, see his classic study *The Good and the Right* (Oxford: Oxford University Press, 1930).

9. Neuenschwander, *Oral History*, 1.

10. Quoted in Wassenaar, 'Ethical Issues', 75.

11. Donald Ritchie, *Doing Oral History* (New York: Twayne Publishers, 1995), 51; Paul Thompson, *The Voice of the Past: Oral History*, 3rd ed. (New York: Oxford University Press, 2000), 254.

12. On resistance to ethical review of research in humanities, see Cribb, 'Ethical Regulation'; Wassenaar, 'Ethical Issues', 63–66.

13. Robert Townsend and Mériam Belli, 'Oral History and IRBs: Caution Urged as Rule Interpretations Vary Widely', *Perspectives* 42, no. 9 (December 2004); Robert Townsend, Carl Ashley, Mériam Belli, Richard Bond and Elizabeth Fairhead, 'Oral History and Review Boards: Little Gain and More Pain', *Perspectives* 44, no. 2 (February 2006). On IRBs and oral history, see also Linda Shopes, 'Institutional Review Boards Have a Chilling Effect on Oral History', *AHA Perspectives* 38, no. 6 (September 2000): 54; Donald Ritchie, 'Institutional Review Boards and Oral History', *Oral History Association Newsletter* 35 (Fall 2001): 4; Neuenschwander, *Oral History*, 47–51.

14. Center for Advanced Study, University of Illinois, *Improving the System for Protecting Human Subjects: Counteracting IRB 'Mission Creep': The Illinois White Paper*, 2004, 4. http://www.law.uiuc.edu/conferences/whitepaper/papers/SSRN-id902995. pdf, accessed 10 May 2008.

15. Tom L. Beauchamp and James F. Childress, *Principles of Biomedical Ethics* (New York: Oxford University Press, 2001).

16. Quoted by Alison Dyer, 'Indigenous Rights' (Open Forum paper, Monte Carlo, 3–6 November 1999). http://www.ficpi.org/library/montecarlo99/indigenous. html, accessed 10 May 2008.

17. I would like to express my gratitude to my colleagues Julia Wells (Rhodes University) and Sekgothe Mokgoatsana (University of the North) for their input on this point.

18. Section 40 of the *Freedom of Information Act of 2000* stipulates that the disclosure of personal information to the public should be prevented when it is likely to cause 'damage or distress'.

19. Wassenaar, 'Ethical Issues', 68.
20. Otsile Ntsoane, 'Intellectual Property Rights and Natural Resources: Some Case Studies amongst Arts and Farming Communities in the North-West Province, South Africa' (paper prepared for the International Workshop on Intellectual Property Rights and Indigenous Knowledge Systems, University of Botswana, 26–28 November 2003).
21. For this section, while taking into account the South African context, I rely on 'Principles and Standards of the Oral History Association' in Neuenschwander, *Oral History*; Ward, 'Oral History Society Ethical Guidelines'.
22. Australian Psychological Society, 'Guidelines for the Provision of Psychological Services and for the Conduct of Psychological Research with Aborigines and Torres Strait Islander People of Australia', May 2003, 7. This document is posted on the Australian Psychological Society's website, but is accessible only to its members. I express my gratitude to Douglas Wassenaar who drew my attention to this document.
23. Neuenschwander, *Oral History*, 33; Hugo Slim and Paul Thompson, *Listening for a Change: Oral Testimony and Development* (London: Panos Publications, 1993), 61.
24. Thompson, *Voice of the Past*, 253–54.
25. Robert Amdur, *Institutional Review Board Member Handbook* (Sudbury, MA: Jones & Bartlett, 2003).
26. Neuenschwander, *Oral History*, 29; Thompson, *Voice of the Past*, 254.
27. See the *Copyright Act 98 of 1978*, as amended, Chapter 1, section 2(2): 'A work, except a broadcast or programme-carrying signal, shall not be eligible for copyright unless the work has been written down, recorded, represented in digital data or signals and otherwise reduced to a material form.'
28. Ward, *Is Your Oral History Legal and Ethical?*
29. Ritchie speaks in this context of a 'relatively small number of words' (*Doing Oral History*, 51); Neuenschwander, of a 'fair use of interviews' (*Oral History*, 34–35); Ward, of 'insubstantial extracts' (*Is Your Oral History Legal and Ethical?*).
30. *Copyright Act 98 of 1978*, as amended, Chapter 1, section 12(3).
31. Australian Psychological Society, 'Guidelines', 5.
32. For more on dealing with this issue, see Chapter 7.
33. Emanuel et al., 'Clinical Research in Developing Countries', 933.
34. See Ward, 'Oral History Society Ethical Guidelines', 3.5 and 3.6.
35. To be defamed, an individual must be alive. Nobody can libel or slander a dead person.
36. Ward, *Is Your Oral History Legal and Ethical?*
37. This raises an important point: if the researcher knows that the material to be discussed is of a legally sensitive nature, the informed consent process must inform all interviewees that the researcher could indeed be forced to make such disclosures in court.

38. Ruth Macklin, ' "Due" and "Undue" Inducements: On Paying Money to Research Subjects', *IRB: A Review of Human Subjects* 3, no. 5 (May 1981): 1–6; Christine Grady et al., 'An Analysis of US Practices of Paying Research Participants', *Contemporary Clinical Trials* 26 (2005): 365–75; Ezekiel J. Emanuel, 'Undue Inducement in Clinical Research in Developing Countries: Is it a Worry?', *The Lancet* 366 (2005): 336–40. I thank Douglas Wassenaar for having drawn my attention to these publications.
39. Thompson, *Voice of the Past*, 256.
40. For more on this process, see Chapter 2 and Appendix 1.

4

The Truth of Tales

Oral Testimony and Teaching History in Schools[1]

CYNTHIA KROS AND NICOLE ULRICH

THIS CHAPTER IS a product of ongoing work that we have been conducting in the province of Mpumalanga at the request of the Mpumalanga Education Department, which seeks to equip social science and history teachers with the requisite skills for teaching the new curriculum, particularly in the field of oral history. In the course of this work, we have confronted enormously complex issues relating to truth and memory, which we contend that the new curriculum has underestimated. The long-standing debates over these issues are not easily resolved, especially under the pressure of the new assessment guidelines for teachers. Although the current curriculum emphasises that credit should be given for critical and interpretive skills, most teachers have been schooled in an empiricist approach to history and still expect to award marks for the 'right' answers. Even given the curriculum's more relativist approach, it still requires learners to demonstrate that they are capable of selecting the most 'reliable' source for a particular event. At this stage of our work, we certainly do not feel that we have all the answers to the many questions that present themselves, but in this chapter, we draw attention to some of the issues that often arise in the teaching and learning of oral history practices.

85

The beginning: The History Workshop

Our work on oral history is based in the History Workshop at the University of the Witwatersrand, which was created by a group of academics who wanted to democratise history in a country that was apparently inextricably caught in the stranglehold of apartheid.[2] The worker militancy of the early 1970s and the student insurgency of the middle of the same decade encouraged these academics to think that history could play a part in radical social transformation. At about the same time, Paul Thompson was offering oral history as a challenge 'to the accepted myths of history' and to the 'authoritarian judgment inherent in its tradition'.[3] Thompson argues that oral history can radically transform the social meaning of history. In common with many other such projects in South Africa, the History Workshop believed that oral history, through its deference to ordinary people, could produce history that was not elitist. The Workshop's ambition was to scour the nooks and crannies of an authoritarian system to reveal those who were forced to take refuge there. It recognised that they devised their own crafty schemes for survival or revenge, which surfaced in what Cobb and Sennett memorably refer to as 'the hidden injuries of class'.[4]

In a survey of the History Workshop's endeavours over the first decade of its existence, Paul la Hausse remarks that the rich veins of oral tradition available to researchers elsewhere on the continent were much more difficult to excavate here.[5] Thus, the social historians who identified with the Workshop tended to accumulate vast transcripts of oral testimonies upon which they based their arguments, which are still surprising in their subtlety and nuance. Many of the historians associated with the Workshop reflected on the difficulties of translating testimonies from people whose graphic visualisation of the past differed so fundamentally from the narrative form in which historians were required to render it.[6] But many scholars were reticent about their methodology or assumed, even at the expense of some discomfort, that they owed it to their subjects to make the narrative intelligible where there were gaps, or to correct its errors.

In the late 1990s, two historians from the Western Cape, Gary Minkley and Ciraj Rassool, delivered a critique of what they rather loosely referred to as the 'social historians'[7] and imputed to them – perhaps unfairly – political motives for refusing to tackle some of the difficult questions that oral history raises.[8] However, there are aspects of their critique that are worth highlighting in the light of new understandings of oral history projects. They criticised what they saw as the reiteration of a dominant resistance narrative, praising one of the Workshop's founders, Belinda Bozzoli, for her uncharacteristic attempt to break the bounds of the traditional narrative in her study *Women of Phokeng*. Co-authored with Mmantho Nkotsoe, Bozzoli's work is based on a series of thematic interviews with female migrant labourers.[9] Minkley and Rassool maintained that few other social historians demonstrated a commitment to examining the relations of power 'embedded' in oral history transactions or to abandoning the 'grand narrative'.[10]

Probably the most productive part of Minkley and Rassool's critique is their observation that social historians have failed to theorise memory. Since the 1980s, there has been a growing interest in memory as a concept that is distinct from history and more than an empirically verifiable remembrance.[11] Although the new discourse on memory is closely associated with what has been called the linguistic turn and the move towards postmodernism, oral historians have generally started paying closer attention to the nature of memory and its relationship to history. This is evident in the work of historians such as Ronald Grele and Alessandro Portelli.[12] Prior to this, social historians, with some notable exceptions, appeared invariably to defer to the hierarchical superiority of documentary evidence. This was true even though the grand old man of oral history in Africa, Jan Vansina, warned that *all* evidence gleaned from one source, whatever its nature, should be regarded as 'on probation'.[13] Helen Bradford, a second-generation social historian, gives the fastidiousness of her mostly male colleagues short shrift when she writes in the introduction to her book on the history of the Industrial and Commercial Workers'

Union: 'much of the testimony of blacks who lived through the 1920s is as reliable as the words of whites now enshrined in archives and publications'.[14]

It might be argued at this point that academic debate and critical reflection cannot have much relevance for schoolteachers wrestling with the demands of the new curriculum. Originally we thought it was enough to teach people about the etiquette of doing oral history. We devised exercises about the technicalities involved in composing questions, allowing for the free flow of the interviewee's narrative and the importance of transcribing it accurately. But, as we explain below, it soon became obvious that we would have to engage with theoretical issues if we were really to help teachers realise the potential of the new curriculum.

As Bozzoli recalls, the History Workshop tried to reach out beyond the 'simply academic' from the outset.[15] Public lectures were combined with 'non-literary forms', such as film and theatre, to make up the 'popular side' of the Workshop's early programmes. By 1984, because of the growing assertiveness of black trade unionism, Bozzoli surmised that the audience had been able to 'take over' and popular intellectuals were enabled to speak out.[16] From the late 1980s, the history curriculum started to be debated and negotiated and Sue Krige and Luli Callinicos, both History Workshop members, decided to broaden its outreach programme to include schoolteachers.

The teachers' workshops continued into the 1990s, heralded by Mandela's release from prison and the imminent collapse of apartheid – a different era from that which Bozzoli describes when the History Workshop's Open Days brought fleets of buses to the university campus. Instead of contesting the official history promoted by the apartheid state, it became possible to engage with participants from state departments, such as the reconstituted Department of Education. After Krige left the university in the late 1990s, there was a brief hiatus in the teachers' workshops, but they were revived at the beginning of the 2000s.

The new curriculum

By 1997, the cumbersome 'Curriculum 2005', representing many points of political compromise, had made its way into the *Government Gazette*. This curriculum seriously threatened the character of history through its creation of the human and social sciences learning area, which brought history and geography together into a bland broth that did justice to neither subject. Fortunately, history was rescued by the second African National Congress (ANC) Minister of Education, Kader Asmal. He had a personal fondness for history, as well as faith in its powers to instil democratic values in the nation's children.

The present curriculum owes much to Asmal's shrewd revision of 'Curriculum 2005', with the help of an investigative commission headed by former education professor, Linda Chisholm. The commission found that 'Curriculum 2005' was much too difficult to implement. The fundamental outcomes-based approach that had been adopted as a basis for 'Curriculum 2005' was preserved, but simplified and rendered into more accessible language. From Grades R (preschool) to 9, history was categorised under social sciences. However, although it still shared this learning area with geography, both subjects were given their own set of independent learning outcomes, related assessment standards and a separate 'knowledge focus'. Teachers were advised to make their own links between the two disciplines. For Grades 10–12, history was restored as a completely autonomous subject.

History in the new curriculum (now known as the 'Revised National Curriculum Statement') is conceived of as having Constitutional obligations. Clearly, it is meant to impart tolerance, an appreciation of diversity and the importance of human rights. It also seems to reflect various influences from the academy, which it may have received through the fairly conscientious process of consultation with the public at large, which preceded its final publication. In terms of history, it is important to note that the new curriculum is preoccupied with helping learners to evaluate various kinds of historical sources. It is permeated with the idea that 'formerly subjugated voices' must be heard[17] and emphasises the value of oral history and 'Indigenous Knowledge Systems' (IKS).[18]

There is much for progressive educators and historians to applaud in the new curriculum. At the teachers' conference on oral history in the curriculum held in Gauteng in 2003,[19] however, one of the Workshop's members, Peter Lekgoathi, sounded an early word of caution. He noted that there is no acknowledgement of how difficult it is to record, let alone collate and interpret, the voices of the 'subjugated'.[20] Oral history, argued Lekgoathi, could not be considered a quick fix for the long indifference of apartheid, which overlooked the history of the vast majority. Lekgaothi was echoing Tedlock's warning not to think of oral history only in terms of confirming or dismissing dominant ideologies.[21] Subsequently, our experiences in running teachers' workshops for the Mpumalanga Department of Education have challenged our ideas about oral history even more profoundly and forced us to examine the vexed issues surrounding memory and historical truth.

Oral history in the classroom has been fairly well established internationally, if only as a means to liven up the subject and to give students a greater sense of an event or period. Jerry Hlabangane, an Mpumalanga teacher, similarly commented on the power of oral history to revive the 'deadwood' subject.[22] The benefits of student-generated oral history research have also been documented and, according to Grace Huerta and Leslie Flemmer, it allows students to participate actively in the learning process and to develop their enquiry and language skills (both verbal and written).[23] Lee Penyak and Pamela Duray argue that the collection and analysis of oral testimonies give students a 'sense of participation in history', and, by capturing human experience, provide the means through which to promote empathy and an understanding of social issues.[24] The significance of this in the South African context is obvious and, as we have seen above, is reinforced in the new curriculum.

However, as we have already suggested, oral history is nowhere near as simple as it may seem at first glance. It places an additional burden on teachers, especially those who are already severely constrained by the lack of resources in their schools, not to mention the teachers who are understandably intimidated by the intricate demands of the new assessment policy. Once we considered learner assessment, which is supposed to drive the new curriculum, we realised that we had to confront some of the tricky issues relating to truth and verification.

What is oral history?

We needed to clearly define oral history for teachers. We settled on the following definition: oral history means history that is passed down by word of mouth. Very simply, we might say that there are two types of oral evidence. The first includes oral testimony, eyewitness or first-hand accounts of events or situations that occurred during the lifetime of the person interviewed. The informant tells a story about him- or herself, about what he or she has seen, heard or done in the past. The second type of oral evidence is oral tradition, which includes stories, praise songs, genealogies or narratives that have been handed down by word of mouth from one generation to the next.[25] Subsequently we discovered that even the apparently simple oral traditions that we had collected for teachers, especially those about succession struggles between contestants to the throne in pre-colonial times, still caused great controversy.[26] Our definition was clearly inadequate.

The History Workshop has generally encouraged the use of life history interviews – interviews conducted with one person focusing on his/her individual life history or family history. Often the interviewee talks about his/her parents, siblings and relatives. The idea is to have a deeper understanding of the individual's life chronologically. By focusing on the life stories of individuals and their families, we are able to gain a better understanding of the experiences of people who are usually ignored (such as peasants, tenants and labourers) and to investigate broader historical themes.[27] These can include the history of land possession and dispossession, identity and acculturation, and religious affiliations. One of the main strengths of life history interviews is that they yield unexpected data. Philip Bonner and Alan Mabin did not think it would be possible to speak to anyone who had lived and worked through the 1918 flu epidemic and the 1920 miners' strike in Pilgrim's Rest. However, oral testimony revealed that the local mining company, Transvaal General Mining Estates, recruited and employed children, who were now adults and able to speak about these events. One of the interviewees, Christian Silikane, had worked on the mines as a child in 1919 and he recalled that there were many young boys working on the stopes at that time.[28]

In our work with teachers, we also suggest using structured and semi-structured interviews. In a structured interview, the researcher prepares all the questions before the interview and only asks these questions (see Appendix 4 for an example). A semi-structured interview is more open than a standardised questionnaire. A few questions are prepared in advance in order to steer the interview, but the interviewees are allowed to give unrestricted answers and the interviewer follows up with related questions. The difficulty with structured and semi-structured interviews is that the interviewer may steer the informant away from important areas that may reveal new data and may also make informants feel that their experiences are unimportant. Nevertheless, making use of structured interviews may be more suitable for learners in the lower grades.

Our workshop experiences

Our conference dealing specifically with oral history and the curriculum in July 2003 was attended by about 120 teachers, mostly from Gauteng. The conference was centred on Constitution Hill, the Constitutional Court and museum complex that has been remodelled within Johannesburg's notorious Fort and associated prisons on the edge of Hillbrow. We attempted to define oral history (see above) and to point to the various methodological challenges that learners and teachers are bound to encounter when they conduct and analyse interviews. By examining the oral testimonies of former prisoners that had been collected by the museum, we demonstrated the unique value of hearing about the experiences of a range of people who had been imprisoned in the dark and terrifying cells of Number Four or the women's jail. No second-hand account could capture the poignancy of, for example, how much a glimpse of the sky meant for a prison inmate.

Facilitators also linked the collection of oral testimonies to the construction and representation of public history, which has entered the new school curriculum, particularly in the Further Education and Training (FET) band – that is, Grades 10–12. This allowed us to contemplate the connections between memory and place. The museum's Mapping Memory Project recalled prisoners to the site, so as 'to give material form to memories that have been made fragile by the passage of time'.[29] Not all prisoners could undergo this process, however, since the Awaiting Trial Block had been demolished to make way for the new Constitutional Court building, leaving only the stairwells, standing like ghostly sentinels on Constitution Square. Former political prisoner Joseph Gogo Khoza recalled the impact this had on him: 'My grief is that we are dealing with a situation that is so altered. The building as I knew it when we were imprisoned here is gone and the most significant thing about our stay here. I am not angry, but it is simply not here and its absence means that the story of the Fort is not complete.'[30] For Khoza, the destruction of the 'material form' has damaged the narrative of the Fort and reduced the significance of his prison experience. Far from feeling the joy or exultation we might have expected when he discovered that the prison had been razed, he felt the intimate sentiment of 'grief' at its loss. The architects of its demolition had obviously anticipated grief and anger and sought to deflect it by explaining on a plaque on one of the surviving stairwells how they had preserved various relics of the Awaiting Trial Block and had dismantled it brick by brick, so as to reassemble it behind the chamber in the Court.

In 2004, the History Workshop was invited to conduct oral history workshops in the more rural provinces of North West and Mpumalanga to help teachers to implement the new curriculum provisions for oral and local history. These workshops were more intensive than the one we had hosted in our own province and were conducted over two days. The number of teachers tended to be smaller, at around thirty or forty. Subsequently, the History Workshop was able to develop a partnership with the Mpumalanga Education Department, particularly with Ian Steenkamp, deputy-chief education specialist for the General Education and Training (GET) band and, later, with Calvin Buthelezi for the FET band.

Much of Mpumalanga's history is fairly obscure, although some academic studies are now more accessible.[31] However, vast areas, especially of the province's township history, remain unexplored. The Grades 4 and 5 curriculum encourages the inclusion of local and provincial history and this seemed to excite many teachers. Most of the oral history projects that they proposed initially involved creating a history of a specific township. As facilitators, we tried to encourage the life history approach, arguing that it enabled us to investigate specific local events and processes and also to evoke broader historical themes, such as the history of land tenure, dispossession, resistance and the construction of identities in several senses – all themes that are endorsed in the curriculum. We also tended to follow the kinds of guidelines outlined in Thompson's classic guide for oral history work in the classroom.[32]

At the Pilgrim's Rest workshop in 2004, we were confronted by the ethical problems attendant on interviewing people who have traumatic histories from which they are still suffering. We realised that we would have to be clear that we were not able to compensate them in any form and that we would have to develop a code of ethics and accountability to our informants.[33] In an exhibition on the Number Four site at the old Fort, described above, Khaya Isaac Magi, who painted an inferno-like representation of the prisoners being humiliated by the guards, has written: 'I am still trying to overcome my prison experiences and I found that by painting these, I am able to share the load with more people.' Magi's testimony suggests that he expected that through recalling and reconstructing his experience, he would find relief from the burden of his nightmarish memory. But some of our Pilgrim's Rest interviewees appeared to have given up hope of transcending the experiences that had caused them pain and we were distressed by our inability 'to share the load'.

In an interview with Ronald Grele, Studs Terkel, author of the famous *Hard Times* (a collection of oral testimonies from the Great Depression in the United States) said of people he had interviewed: 'It's their truth. So if it's their truth, it's got to be my truth; it's their experiences. Somebody lived through that time with a certain something he remembers, that scar left on him; the memory is true.'[34] But Grele insists that we should not abdicate our role as historians or, in this case, our role in teaching other people to become historians. Historians are committed to a special way of looking at the world and must be capable of 'methodological introspection'.[35]

Later in the same workshop, we addressed the teachers on assessment and discovered that many of them had not yet been exposed to the new assessment criteria prescribed by the curriculum. In the end, this turned out to be a blessing in disguise because as we were forced to deconstruct every assessment standard at every level of the curriculum, so we had to isolate necessary historical skills. Naturally this took a long time – certainly much longer than the Pilgrim's Rest workshop – and, to some extent, we are still engaged in the process. We initially approached it thus: outcomes-based education is centred on the idea that the most important goals of education should be the development and growth of learners. It's important to think about what we are setting out to enable our learners *to do*. How do we realise the critical, developmental and learning outcomes? Will learners be able to apply the knowledge and skills expressed in the outcomes?[36] We identified the critical outcomes in the GET band that appear to relate most to oral history as those that say learners should be enabled to:

- work as members of an effective team or community;
- organise work effectively;
- collect information, organise and analyse it, and finally evaluate it;
- communicate what has been learned and understood effectively; and
- understand the world better.[37]

The developmental outcomes in the GET band that we saw as most relevant to oral history work are those that say learners should be enabled to:

- learn more effectively;
- become more effective, active citizens;
- appreciate many different aspects of the environment (including art and culture); and
- work well in the contemporary world of work.[38]

As far as the social sciences (history) curriculum goes, we maintained that it was important to note that we are aiming to develop the learners'

- enquiry skills;
- historical understanding; and
- ability to interpret sources.[39]

These outcomes are also applicable to the FET band, although, of course, the assessment standards that accompany every outcome make it clear that learners from Grades 10–12 should be able to demonstrate skills and concepts at a higher level than those at the more junior levels. In addition, there is another outcome (learning outcome 4) for the FET band that encourages us to help learners 'to engage critically with issues around heritage'.[40]

Working with teachers impressed upon us how important it is to think through the stages of development and to support learners and encourage growth. These are the kinds of questions we asked to help us to focus on achieving the outcomes:

- How do we find out if learners are gaining new skills, knowledge and understanding?
- How do we help them to communicate more clearly and to develop different kinds of communication (explanation, narrative, debate, graphical and diagrammatic forms)?

What we have tried to do is to work with teachers to draw up the stages of an oral history project, designing assessment activities at every step. They need not all be formal assessments. For example, learners might be helped through teacher guidance and peer assessment to find suitable subjects to interview, to make up a series of suitable questions to ask, and to check whether or not their record of the interview is accurate. We recommend formal assessment for the way in which learners have applied the information they have found. We advised teachers to be very clear about what kinds of application they are looking for and also about how the learners' work will be assessed. In line with current assessment policy, we maintained that it is best to talk through assessment criteria with the learners beforehand.

We reminded teachers that it is important to keep track of the process, being aware that a learner may apparently do all the right things, but still end up with what may be seen as a weak interview. The learner should not be penalised for this immediately, we have argued, but with the aid of formative assessment should be encouraged to think of the next stage or remediation (for example, conducting a second interview with the same informant). Summative assessment (that is, for marks) should really only take place at the end of the whole process.

In addition to the outcomes that accommodate the creative use of oral history in the classroom, there are some content areas that similarly encourage its deployment. In the Senior Phase (Grades 7–

9), there are 'knowledge foci' on several wars in which South Africans were involved or which had an impact on South Africa. We feel that the curriculum encourages us to look at how these wars affected people, reflecting the curriculum's emphasis on the history of people's experiences. When one goes out into the local environment and asks questions about what happened during a particular war, it might be that the answers are unexpected, but convey the significance of the war and why it still matters today.

Three case studies

Case study 1: The township veteran

Jerry Hlabangane, one of the teachers at the Mpumalanga workshop, eager to translate his training into practice, was intrigued by the stories that surrounded one of his neighbours, octogenarian Jeremiah Mdalane, a veteran of the Second World War.[41] Hlabangane used the life history method, asking open-ended questions of *Mkhulu* (Grandpa) Mdalane. In late 2006, Hlabangane reflected that, despite some of the obstacles he had encountered, he had 'learned a lot'. When questioned as to the content of his learning, he gave this answer:

> I expected the stories to confirm, for example, the myth that black soldiers received only jackets and bicycles while white soldiers were given land. That's not the truth. White soldiers of the same rank received nothing – it was only the senior ranks. I expected that hate feeling. Black soldiers were thought of as auxiliaries to dig trenches, carry wounded. My informant said that he was involved in combat. In military camps segregation was not there. They were treated in the same hospital, in the same ward. But they were not only South African soldiers. He was in the British Army . . . I expected what I knew. I was expecting segregation in the camps.[42]

The statement 'I expected what I knew' is striking. Mdalane's testimony confounded what Hlabangane thought he knew about segregation and racial hatred. It also appeared to contradict the narrative of the post-1994 textbooks and those of several other testimonies from veterans. Mdalane told a completely different story that continued into civilian life when he was deployed as a policeman in Soweto. At one stage, it appears from his testimony, he was involved in disciplining the notorious thugs from Basutoland known as 'the Russians'.[43] When Hlabangane asked him what he would do 'if the war came again', the old man replied: 'Yes, I can go back.' He talked, Hlabangane recalls, 'about how he has to stay at home now and can't defend the people he loves from those who come to kill them'.[44] Clearly, in this instance, Hlabangane's interviewee was using the past to comment on the present and the war of 60 years ago was still vivid for him.

Hlabangane has consistently raised the issue of how to validate oral sources. He has spent a substantial amount of time trying to verify *Mkhulu* Mdalane's testimony. The locally based soldiers who served with him were no longer alive and Hlabangane had to use documents, including letters and certificates, to confirm what he was told. But the documentation was sparse. Along the way, he also gained first-hand experience in negotiating access with cagey gatekeepers. As a Jehovah's Witness, Mdalane's wife is prohibited from discussing war and Hlabangane had to obtain permission from her church before he was allowed to interview her. He was less successful in securing an interview with the Major-General of the Nelspruit military base. After a laborious bureaucratic process, he was refused an appointment. As he remarked ruefully, 'Verification was tough.'[45]

As we have pointed out above, Hlabangane's interviewee was using the past to comment on the present. In the present, he is an old man who, Hlabangane remarks, walks with difficulty and who feels his powerlessness (presumably against the actions of criminals) acutely. But, in the most recent interview conducted with Hlabangane, we may also observe how the latter's own patterns of 'then and now' intersect with those of his informant. Hlabangane, like his informant, rejects a simple, binary (black and white) account of racial segregation.

A couple of years ago, he returned to teach at his old school in the township of Kanyamazane. In the course of outlining his plans for promoting oral history at the school, he recalled his white teachers, two of whom still work there. He pointed out that during the period of boycotts and riots in the 1980s, 'we defended our white teachers unlike the other schools'.[46] 'The boys secured the fence,' he explains. Despite racial segregation, most obviously manifested in the compartmentalisation of the staffroom in those days, which Hlabangane notes, he feels that he owes the white teachers a debt of gratitude. Nowadays, he says, he gets angry when the students are rude to the white teachers. An oral history of the school, he feels, might help its learners to recognise the contribution made by the white teachers and to inaugurate the principal's vision of a school 'renaissance'.

Both Hlabangane and his informant look to the past as a time in which they felt empowered and validated, refer to an intermediate or present time of disillusionment and decline and implicitly look forward to a rebirth. They are drawn to the past, not in a nostalgic sense, which implies defeatism, but as a potential reservoir of resources for taking on the challenges of the present.[47] The old man walks with difficulty, but he keeps on walking, recalling that the doctors at the army hospital told him after he was wounded that he would lose his mobility if he did not.[48]

What we are doing here is applying some of the critical ideas on memory to what Hlabangane relates about his experiences with his interviewee. In foraging for the deeper meaning of the narrative and by locating its high and low points, we have teased out much more than a set of data.[49] We are observing what Frisch described as people living with their history over time.[50] Both Mdalane and Hlabangane create 'patterns' out of their historical memories. In the words of Frisch, they become 'cultural documents' with their own intrinsic value.[51]

Before saying what we think this means for the teaching of oral history, we should pause to reflect on the actions of the person who is interviewing the interviewer (Cynthia Kros). She starts the September 2006 interview by setting up the life history format, perhaps subconsciously casting the mould for the memory patterns – the then-and-now themes – which Hlabangane will shortly begin to weave. 'Tell me about yourself . . . what attracted you to history? How did you choose your topic? What have you learned from your project?' and so on. 'The minute you ask a question,' Benison observes, 'you have a bias . . . your bias says: "Gee, that's important." '[52] Kros then elaborates on the themes that she hears about racial co-operation, reciprocity and reconciliation. At the same time, she must rely heavily on Hlabangane to explain the history and character of Kanyamazane, of which she is totally ignorant. Suddenly the leader of the oral history workshop, the academic from the university, must change places with the learner-teacher. This happens several times in the course of the interview. One moment, Kros is drawing the meaning out of Hlabangane's narrative in ways that he might not expect; in the next moment, she is obliged to ask him elementary questions about Kanyamazane.

What we would like most for teachers to get out of this case study and their own experiences is the sheer joy of listening to and telling stories. The stories also tell us about how people make meaning out of history and this also provides the basis for important lessons. Even though there may be literal inaccuracies in people's stories, our interaction with them gives us a finer appreciation of how history is constructed and interpreted.

Case study 2: Assassination or accident

In 2006, one of the History Workshop researchers, Tshepo Moloi, who was working on forced removals, interviewed a certain Mr Maseko, who was a friend and comrade-in-arms of Saul Mkhize, the legendary leader of the resistance against the removals at Driefontein (near Volksrust in Mpumalanga) during the early 1980s. We used Moloi's interview in the second booklet that we wrote for the Mpumalanga oral history project.[53] In April 1983, at the height of the resistance, Mkhize was addressing a crowd of local residents in the grounds of the local primary school when he was killed by a white policeman, who was accompanied by a black colleague. We do not know if Mkhize was shot because the policeman panicked when the crowd seemed to be turning aggressive, or if he was the victim of a premeditated assassination plot. But Maseko had no doubt that Mkhize had been assassinated – since there had already been several failed attempts on his life – and he made this the high point of the narrative that he recounted to Moloi. We had the idea of asking the readers of our booklet to compare the accounts of the incident as they appeared in a contemporary police report, in an eyewitness report compiled by the newspaper *The Rand Daily Mail* and in Maseko's story, as told to Moloi. It seemed like the foundation of a very good exercise for getting learners to think about how we decide which version of a story is the most credible. Moloi had consciously tried to behave as a role model for interviewers. He addressed Maseko respectfully throughout as *Mkhulu* and reflected productively on the idiomatic nature of Maseko's language, which sometimes proved to be a barrier to their communication, even though they both spoke isiZulu.

Maseko's story is powerful and moving, especially when it is placed in juxtaposition with the obviously self-serving police report. He is an extremely skilled narrator and it seems that he is also exhorting us to recognise the value of the history that he has spent a lifetime nurturing, in anticipation of an opportunity to pass it on to a young man like Moloi.[54] From the ways in which he repeats various aspects of his account and periodically checks that Moloi is following, we may deduce that he sees himself as entrusting Moloi with the history of resistance to the removal. This is reminiscent of the way in which Mkhize supposedly sought to entrust the history of black land ownership in the area to 'the youth' of the early 1980s.[55]

This exercise illustrates that often there are no clear answers, but we encourage teachers to believe that debate is good for strengthening necessary historical skills, such as argument and the questioning of evidence. We developed assessment activities that evaluated learners' ability to extract information from the reports and Maseko's story. We guided them by asking questions, such as: who is telling this story and why; are there any gaps or contradictions in these stories; is there anything we find hard to believe in any of the stories, given the position of the crowd, Maseko, and the policemen? The policeman used a shotgun to kill Mkhize. The teachers with whom we have tried the exercise invariably asked if this would have been an appropriate weapon or not for an assassination. They have also pointed out that it would be helpful to know if assassination of political leaders by agents of the police force was common in this period and if the Truth and Reconciliation Commission ever heard evidence relating to this case.

Moloi's interview is very rich. Here too, an examination of the deeper structures of the narrative yields very interesting observations. Maseko piques our interest almost from the outset by suggesting that he is working up to a description of how Mkhize will die. Maseko ensures that Moloi has a mental picture of both the historical and geographical landscape in which the drama will play out. Maseko almost tests Moloi on some of the landmarks that he would have passed on his way to the interview. In his narrative, he invests Mkhize with extraordinary qualities. Undoubtedly, the latter was extremely shrewd and was well educated, legally astute and well connected. His correspondence with government officials and the relevant minister all bear this out. But Maseko endows Mkhize with visionary powers as well, which enabled him, like the Scarlet Pimpernel, to evade capture several times before the fatal school meeting. Maseko then goes to great lengths to flesh out his own presence at the meeting and his proximity to Mkhize.

Maseko dramatises the recall of his memory, by saying that he has forgotten the names of some of the other witnesses and then remembering them before the interview ends. We could conclude that Maseko's memory lets him down at certain points because he is old. But it is more likely that he is deliberately making the 'syntax' of his memory visible (the way in which he summons the memories) because he wants his interlocutor to appreciate the effort he is making to recall this history.[56] The implicit point he is making is that it is a history that has been deeply repressed.

Case study 3: The magical engine

In one of our recent workshops in Middelburg, Mpumalanga, we faced one of our biggest challenges yet. We got into a discussion about the Samora Machel memorial – erected to commemorate the death of the former president of Mozambique and the crew of a Russian aeroplane that crashed on the border of South Africa and Machel's home country in 1986. The suspicion that the aeroplane was lured to its doom by a decoy beacon set up inside what was then apartheid South Africa has not yet been disproved. The teachers were agitated by news that the memorial was to be augmented by an ostentatious amphitheatre and museum complex funded by the province's Department of Public Works. By all accounts, the architect of the memorial, remarkable for its austere simplicity, is also troubled by the planned extension.

The memorial, as it stands, incorporates the wreckage of the plane and the mention of this feature sparked a rapid series of anecdotes about the Machel crash. Teachers recalled stories they had heard about how the Russian pilot, realising that his plane had been sabotaged, wrestled with the controls to ensure that it did not cross the border, but went down in the country that had caused its destruction. They also said they had heard stories about how Machel had not really died in the accident. But the one that received the most attention was the story of how various attempts had been made to transport the engine of the plane to other sites. However, every time it was placed elsewhere, it had begun to run again. The story described the revival of the engine at several different locations, until at last it was returned to the crash site where it evidently found peace. We were all enthralled by this wonderful ghost story and hardly wanted to break the spell. But then one of the teachers asked Peter Delius, who was leading this section of the workshop, what to do with stories that were so blatantly false. He very wisely answered that one should ask why such stories circulated. What were people trying to explain through telling a story like this one? If we are faced with stories like this in the classroom, we should be careful not to dismiss them. We should rather ask questions of our learners about what such stories show about people's attitudes to Machel, as well as their attitudes to the apartheid government.[57]

Learning the tools of the trade

Using his own experiences, Jerry Hlabangane has trained several Grade 11 learners in conducting oral history. The learners, evidently inspired by their teacher's passion and dedication, competed at a national level with distinction. We have come full circle to the History Workshop's first workshop for teachers, where Lekgoathi warned that oral sources should not be used as a quick fix. Our experiences have demonstrated how complex both oral testimony and oral tradition can be and how much critical reflection they require. Teachers used to working within a positivist paradigm have found the shifts required in dealing with oral sources very taxing. It is impossible to provide a simple checklist by which to judge the truth of oral sources, since truth is highly elusive. This need not be a stumbling block, however. Indeed, the tricky pursuit of truth hones the skills of debate and analysis germane to the discipline of history. More than that, oral sources put us in touch with worldviews and experiences far removed from our own. We maintain that this conception of history is in line with the intentions of the authors of the national school curriculum. However, teachers need much more support to achieve the potential latent in the new curriculum.

Notes

1. This chapter is based on a paper presented at 'Dancing with Memory: International Oral History Conference', Sydney, Australia, 2006. We would like to acknowledge here the centrality of Jerry Hlabangane to the process of thinking about oral history in the classroom, as well as the contributions of our colleagues in the History Workshop, University of the Witwatersrand. Thanks also to Cynthia's writing group for helpful commentary.

2. The History Workshop was certainly not the only research institution in South Africa to collect oral testimony or, indeed, to conduct workshops for teachers, as the other chapters in this book demonstrate.

3. Paul Thompson, *The Voice of the Past* (Oxford: Oxford University Press, 1978), 18.

4. Quoted in Ronald Grele, 'Movement without Aim', in *The Art of Oral History*, 2nd ed., ed. Ronald Grele (Chicago: Precedent Publishing, 1985), 28.

5. Paul la Hausse, 'Oral History and the South African Historians', *Radical History Review* 46, no. 7 (Winter 1990).

6. See, for example, Tim Keegan, *Facing the Storm: Portraits of Black Lives in South Africa* (London: Zed Press, 1988), 161.

7. We take this to be a reference to historians working on History Workshop principles: 'history from below' as opposed to the 'Great Man' approach and other ways of writing about oral history.

8. Gary Minkley and Ciraj Rassool, 'Orality, Memory and Social History in South Africa', in *Negotiating the Past: The Making of Memory in South Africa*, ed. Sarah Nuttall and Carli Coetzee (Cape Town: Oxford University Press, 1998).

9. Belinda Bozzoli, with Mmantho Nkotsoe, *Women of Phokeng: Consciousness, Life Strategy and Migrancy in South Africa, 1900–1983* (London: James Currey, 1991).

10. Minkley and Rassool, 'Orality, Memory', 94–95.

11. Kerwin Lee Klein, 'On the Emergence of Memory in Historical Discourse', *Representations, Special Issue: Grounds for Remembering* 69 (Winter 2000): 127–50.

12. Grele, ed., *The Art of Oral History*; Alessandro Portelli, *The Death of Luigi Trastulli and Other Stories: Form and Meaning in Oral History* (Albany: State University of New York Press, 1991).

13. Quoted in Thompson, *Voice of the Past*, 210.

14. Helen Bradford, *A Taste of Freedom: The ICU in Rural South Africa, 1924–1930* (New Haven: Yale University Press, 1987), xiv.

15. Belinda Bozzoli, 'Intellectuals, Audiences and Histories', *Radical History Review* 46, no. 7 (Winter 1990): 242–43.

16. Ibid., 249.

17. 'Revised National Curriculum Statement, Grades R–10 (Schools) Policy' (Pretoria: Government Printer, 2003), 9.

18. 'Indigenous Knowledge Systems' refer to the way in which indigenous knowledge was constituted and interacted with colonial forms of knowledge.

19. The teachers' workshops were revived in 2002, starting with a workshop on 'Teaching Apartheid'. This was followed in 2003 with the conference on 'Oral Testimony and Teaching History'.

20. Peter Lekgoathi, 'Voices of Our Past: Oral Testimony and Teaching History' (keynote address delivered to History Workshop's annual workshop for teachers, 2003), in *Educator's Guide to the UNESCO General History of Africa (for the FET Curriculum)*, ed. J. Bam and C. Dyer (Cape Town: New Africa Education for the Ministry of Education, 2004).

21. Dennis Tedlock, 'Oral History as Poetry', in *The Art of Oral History*, 2nd ed., ed. Ronald Grele (Chicago: Precedent Publishing, 1985), 203.

22. Interview with Jerry Hlabangane by Cynthia Kros, September 2006.

23. Grace Huerta and Leslie Flemmer, 'Using Student-Generated Oral History Research in the Secondary Classroom', *Social Studies* 91, no. 3 (2000).

24. Lee Penyak and Pamela Duray, 'Oral History and Problematic Questions Promote Issue Centered Education', *Social Studies* 90, no. 2 (1999).

25. Philip Bonner, Cynthia Kros, Peter Lekgoathi, Helen Ludlow, Sellow Mathabatha, Katie Mooney, Noor Nieftagodien, Nicole Ulrich, Ian Steenkamp and Wanga Tabata, 'Oral History: A Guide for Educators', pamphlet published by the Mpumalanga Department of Education, 2005. Available from the Mpumalanga Department of Education or from the History Workshop, http://web.wits.ac.za/Academic/Humanities/SocialSciences/HistoryWorkshop/Training.htm, accessed 21 May 2008.

26. At our most recent Mpumalanga workshop in February 2007, we discovered that two different oral traditions concerning the contest between Hlubi and Dlamini for the kingship in the area of present-day Swaziland two centuries ago were still capable of stimulating vigorous debate among the participants who identified with one or other of the parties.

27. Bonner et al., 'Oral History: A Guide for Educators'.

28. Interview with Christian Silikane by Phil Bonner and Alan Mabin, February 1985.

29. Constitution Hill, text on site.

30. Constitution Hill, text on exhibit at No. 4.

31. See, for example, Peter Delius, ed., *Mpumalanga: History and Heritage* (Pietermaritzburg: University of KwaZulu-Natal Press, 2007).

32. Thompson, *Voice of the Past*.

33. The University of the Witwatersrand has developed a set of ethical protocols for researchers in the social sciences. See Philippe Denis, 'Oral History in a Wounded Country', in *Orality, Literacy and Colonialism in South Africa*, ed. Jonathan Draper (Atlanta: Society of Biblical Literature; Pietermaritzburg: Cluster Publications, 2003). Denis argues that it is essential to provide feedback to communities and individuals involved in the interviewing process: 'In a wounded country, one does not collect stories merely to satisfy one's curiosity' (5).

34. Quoted in Grele, 'Movement without Aim', 14.

35. Ibid., 204.

36. Bonner et al., 'Oral History: A Guide for Educators'.

37. 'Revised National Curriculum Statement, Grades 7–9 Schools. Senior Phase' (Johannesburg: Department of Education and Gauteng Institute for Educational Development, 2004), 11. Also see http://www.education.gpg.gov.za, accessed 20 May 2008.

38. Ibid., 11.

39. Ibid., 23.

40. 'History Curriculum Statement' (Pretoria: Government Printer, 2003).

41. Interview with Jerry Hlabangane by Cynthia Kros, September 2006.

42. Ibid.

43. See Philip Bonner, 'The Russians on the Reef 1947–57: Urbanisation, Gang Warfare and Ethnic Mobilisation', in *Apartheid's Genesis, 1935–1962*, ed. Philip Bonner, Peter Delius and Deborah Posel (Johannesburg: Ravan Press, 1993).

44. Interview with Jerry Hlabangane by Cynthia Kros, September 2006.

45. Ibid.

46. Ibid.

47. See Grele, 'Movement without Aim', 251, for this meaning of nostalgia.

48. Interview with Jerry Hlabangane by Cynthia Kros, September 2006.

49. Grele, 'Movement without Aim'.

50. Michael Frisch, 'Oral History and *Hard Times*: A Review Essay', in *The Oral History Reader*, ed. Robert Perks and Alistair Thomson (London: Routledge, 1998).

51. Ibid., 36.

52. Grele, 'Movement without Aim', 85.

53. Cynthia Kros, Tshepo Moloi and Nicole Ulrich, 'Activity Manual on Oral History, Grades 4–9' (Johannesburg: History Workshop and Mpumalanga Department of Education, 2006). Unpublished, available from the History Workshop.

54. Grele, 'Movement without Aim', 236–43.

55. According to Maseko, Mkhize called the meeting at which he was shot to explain the history of land tenure to the youth.

56. Denis Hirson, *White Scars: On Reading and Rites of Passage* (Johannesburg: Jacana, 2006), 149.

57. For a discussion of myth in oral history, see Alessandro Portelli, 'What Makes Oral History Different?' in *The Oral History Reader*, ed. Perks and Thomson.

5

'Why Should I Tell My Story?'

Culture and Gender in Oral History

RADIKOBO NTSIMANE

THIS CHAPTER INVESTIGATES the ways in which an interviewee's culture and gender shapes his/her response to an interview situation. Much has been written about culture and gender in oral history.[1] The cultural background of an interviewee will always colour how he/she testifies about his/her history. Similarly, men and women, even within the same culture, do not respond in the same way when they are interviewed. In southern Africa, interviewers are often educated people, particularly those who are participating in a university-sponsored project or working towards a university degree. They are interested in the lives of the interviewees for the knowledge and experiences these people have gained through life. Because of the institutional support they enjoy and their easy access to financial resources, the interviewers tend to be seen by the interviewees as being in a position of power. Although not powerless in the strict sense of the word, interviewees in South Africa seldom recognise that their knowledge is power. The interaction between the interviewees and the interviewers needs to be analysed against this background.

Many of the examples used in this chapter are drawn from my experience as a researcher at the Sinomlando Centre for Oral History and Memory Work in Africa, a research and community development centre at the University of KwaZulu-Natal. The main purpose of

109

this chapter is to bring to the attention of oral history practitioners the importance of the cultural dynamics that shape an interview. Insensitivity to the gender and cultural background of the interviewees and to their social location will limit the value of the interview encounter.

The social location of the interviewee

In African societies, as a result of a long history of patriarchy and male domination, the social location of each individual can strongly shape his or her engagement with the interview process. In particular, men tend to feel that they have greater freedom when they are asked to share their experiences in an interview. Women are more likely to feel inhibited when addressed by a stranger, especially a man. They respond more freely to the questions of women interviewers, even when they are strangers in the community. Women with education and positions of influence in society, such as teachers, nurses, government officials and businesswomen, are more likely to talk openly to male interviewers and less likely to raise suspicion within the community, as their professions require that they interact with strangers.

Likewise, children need to be reassured by their parents or caregivers before agreeing to speak in an interview. Like adults, they only talk in the presence of the people with whom they feel comfortable. African children are taught to leave the company of their parents when a conversation with other adults begins. Writing about his early life in a Zulu chief's home, Albert Luthuli says: '[My grandfather] had a constant stream of visitors, but of course their comings and goings took place well beyond my horizons – the courtesy demanded that when adults came, children disappeared. And the village deliberations, which were conducted in the traditional Zulu manner in the open, were not any affair of a child.'[2] In a Western context, children are more likely to mingle with guests in their homes. In cultures that value secrecy as a protection against envious neighbours and relatives, children are deemed too young to keep secrets. Seen as incomplete human beings, they constitute a risk when entrusted with confidential information.

Generally speaking, African people have difficulties with a member of the community being interviewed privately by a stranger. In a tightly knit community, everybody is constantly under the surveillance of neighbours. There is the perception that somebody who is interviewed privately may divulge, willingly or not, community secrets or incriminating information. An interviewer who insists on interviewing someone individually de facto excludes neighbours and family members from the discussion. The interview may be seen as a gossiping session and the interviewee suspected of harbouring malicious intentions, which may lead to an accusation of witchcraft, since in many communities, a jealous person is seen as potentially being a witch. As Adam Ashforth points out, in an African community, witchcraft is always in the background.[3]

Sometimes, however, some people feel brave enough to talk, even if they risk being accused of gossiping. There are times when it is recognised that it is better to talk about some things. Those accused of evil intentions will make use of the earliest opportunity to clear their names. In such situations, it does not matter to whom they tell the story, as long as it helps them to avoid danger. The goal is to set the record straight or to deal with unfinished business, as Philippe Denis suggests in a paper on oral history in South Africa.[4] Ashforth confirms that people do not easily discuss sensitive matters with neighbours or relatives, but will usually do so when their safety requires that they address the issue. 'The matters of which people speak when they talk of witchcraft,' he writes, 'are of the first importance for their security in everyday life.'[5] Interviewees may want to tell their stories if they think that there is a danger that others may distort them. It does not always happen that the people who have a full knowledge of a story receive the opportunity to talk freely. In any community, powerful people control freedom of speech and decide who is allowed to talk and who is not. However, sometimes if an interview is conducted by a stranger, these restrictions can be more easily negotiated.

Understanding the African worldview

Culture, as understood here, is the way in which a given group of people deals with issues such as health, sexuality, marriage, sport, education and religion in daily life.[6] For the purposes of this chapter, I would add that culture, at least for Africans, is inextricably connected to the spirit world. For most black people, even those who are confessed Christians, the spirit world, which Western people often dismiss as superstition, is a lived reality. Interviews dealing with topics such as misfortune, failure, marriage, sexuality, sickness and death are explained in relation to the spirit world. While such an explanation may seem implausible to Western or Western-trained people, the reality is that in the minds of many interviewees, the spiritual world does indeed control destiny. Isak Niehaus, who conducted interviews in the Mpumalanga province, gives a vivid account of this phenomenon:

> Villagers believed that any sign of success could motivate witchcraft attacks from envious neighbours. For example, soon after Hitekane Manzini, a well-known *ngaka*, started building a new home with money supplied by her daughter, her clientele dwindled. Later Hitekane uncovered a plastic bag, containing *dihlare*, at her gate. She told me the next-door neighbours had buried the *dihlare* to drive her clients away. Similarly, when Florence Nokeri took her ill child to an *ngaka*, she was told that a noise at her home had attracted the attention of her neighbours. Florence asked the *ngaka* whether it could be a music system that her husband had recently purchased. The *ngaka* replied affirmatively. 'Yes. This can make such a sound. Be careful! Your neighbours are on your heels!'[7]

The semantic distance between cultural perspectives can be profound. To be able to understand their interlocutors, interviewers need time and patience. They have to probe the stories again and again to avoid misunderstandings. When there is confusion, the interviewees will bring forth the necessary clarifications if the interviewers are supportive, patient and committed. Trying hard to understand the Zulu worldview, Axel-Ivar Berglund repeatedly asked questions of clarity when he researched his book *Zulu Thought-Patterns and Symbolism*. Here is an example of such patient questioning and probing:

> B[erglund]: But why did *ixhanti* lie on the clay so that you had to move it to get at the clay?
>
> — Because it is the snake of the waters.
>
> B: What does it mean that it is the snake of the waters?
>
> — It means that it is the snake of the waters which gives life. That is why it is called the snake of the waters.
>
> B: Are the waters special waters?
>
> — It is as I said water that is living, running in the river. That is the living water. If the water had been in a dam as you asked (a while ago), then there would not be a snake in it. It is the living waters.
>
> B: I know that the water of men is living because the shades give it life in procreation. Is the water of the pool at all similar to the water of men?
>
> — The water of men is one thing. The water of women is another thing. This water is the water of the woman when she is pregnant. The snake is the one we say is in the woman. Sometimes it eats the children, not letting her give birth. Sometimes it gives them (the children) prosperity. Then they grow and become healthy. It is this water that I am talking of when I speak of the living waters. There are these two living waters, the one of men and the other of women.
>
> B: I know of the snake that women have, but generally it is feared.
>
> — Ah, you said it yourself! Is not the snake of the pool fearful as I have been saying all the time, telling you of its fearfulness! So now you see the combination.[8]

Such can be the rewards of patience, good preparation and respect. Berglund's interviewing method can be applied in other contexts. Oral historians must appreciate how complicated it is for interviewees to share their worldview with people of another culture. Without probing questions, the interviewees may assume incorrectly that the interviewers understand them when, in fact, their meaning is obscure. The difficulties of communication can be compounded when an interviewee makes use of phrases or words that are particular to the culture under examination. It is incumbent upon oral historians to explain the meaning of their words to their readers. In the introduction to her book, *Basali! Stories by and about Women in Lesotho*, Limakatso Kendall thus noted that women in Lesotho address each other as '*Basali*'. This word, which is commonly translated as 'women', has many other meanings when used as an interjection: 'It could be translated as some variant of "You're so sassy/clever/good-looking/ outrageous/hilarious/dangerous/powerful/dazzling/audacious that I don't know what more to say to you."'[9] This richness is embedded in the particular gendered culture of these women and could easily be lost by a less attentive historian.

The language of the interview

Despite the South African government's attempts to promote all of the eleven official languages of South Africa, English continues to dominate in schools, in the media and in public life. Therefore all interviews, if they are to be presented in an academic context, must eventually be translated into English. Most interviewers, even when they are fluent in an African language, prefer to conduct interviews in English. Oral history projects have monetary constraints and the cost of translation is high.

While interviewers may find it easier to work in the language in which they have been trained, many interviewees are reluctant to express their thoughts in a second language and these interviews may suffer in quality because of a lack of adequate vocabulary. Unless they occupy a public position as teachers, priests or politicians and are therefore used to speaking publicly, many African interviewees feel inadequate in an interview situation. They are easily intimidated at the sight of a tape recorder. Using a second language makes the situation more intimidating still.

For these reasons, it is preferable, if possible under financial constraints, to give interviewees the choice of the language and then to budget for translation. Such is the policy of the Sinomlando Centre at the University of KwaZulu-Natal. Belinda Bozzoli[10] and Beverley Haddad[11] used the same method when interviewing women in Phokeng and Vulindlela respectively. Haddad went a step further by reproducing excerpts of interviews in the original isiZulu in her dissertation.[12]

Cultural etiquette

In Africa, there are often strict cultural rules governing how people should relate to each other. Interviewers who ignore these rules may face resistance or rejection. For example, it is a sign of disrespect for children to look adults in the eye. The same applies to women and junior people when they interact with men or senior people. Typically, Brian Khoza, a Zulu journalist who had developed the habit of looking at people in the eye, was advised by his peers that eye contact might be construed by women as flirting.[13]

Handshakes, in particular, have been a source of embarrassment and uncertainty for a long time in intercultural encounters. Interviewees may hold the hand of the interviewer for a long time during the greeting session. Some cultures do not allow women to shake hands with male strangers, while others require a firm handshake. The woman interviewee may be taken by surprise if the greeting session takes a strange turn and may take offence as a result. Similarly, there are constraints set by culture with regard to seating arrangements. Among Zulu people, for example, men and women sit on different sides of the hut, but this rule is not followed in the townships and suburbs. What remains of the traditionally gendered arrangement is the sentiment that men should keep a respectable distance from women or sit where the men are seated. In African societies, space is therefore gendered.[14]

The African understanding of time

Many cultures have different understandings of time. Even so-called African time has many shades. Oral historians engage with time in two ways. First, they must set a date and time to conduct the interview. Second, in their questioning, they ask the interviewee to delve into past time. Both of these tasks will be viewed, for both interviewer and interviewer, through the lens of his or her culture.

Disregarding how the targeted interviewee relates to time can cause problems for an interviewer. When setting up an appointment, it is necessary to establish whether the time agreed upon is specific or approximate. One should inquire if the meeting time is at *exactly* two o'clock, or if it is at *about* two o'clock, or even at *any time after* two o'clock. There are people whose lives and activities are governed by exact timekeeping and they divide their lives strictly by time into activities that are important to them. Other people do not aspire to be so precise in their timing of arrivals and departures. For trust to develop between the interviewer and the interviewee, the time given for the interview must be respected. The interviewer must try to be at the interview location on time. However, the interviewer must exercise patience and wait, in the event that the interviewee arrives late. Should interviewers leave the place before the interviewee arrives, their lack of patience will be seen as lack of genuine interest. If it is important, it surely is worth waiting for.

Often when African people arrive late for an appointment, their tardiness is viewed negatively by people of Western origin. Such critics affirm the stereotype that Africans are inherently incapable of punctuality. They ignore the important fact that the interviewees have many other commitments, while the interviewer's first priority is the scheduled interview. In fact, it is sometimes in the interest of the interviewers that the interviewees arrive late. Their late arrival may be caused by their desire to remove obstacles to the interview. In some cases, it is advisable to make a telephone call in the morning of the interview to confirm the appointment. Should interviewers experience an emergency that will delay them, they must inform the interviewees. This should be done in a polite and professional way and plans made to reschedule the interview.

In oral history, time also features prominently in the content of the interview. Interviewees are asked to remember events and places. 'Conceptions of time in general can be of timeless eternity, of cyclical time and of linear time,' writes Jan Vansina, 'but no culture uses just one of these representations. In Christianity, Islam, and Judaism, the dominant time is linear. Time marches to a resolution of the world into eternity that exists side by side with it.'[15] For example, Sotho and Nguni people see time divided into periods by the major historical events in their lives. Wars and battles, droughts and famines, and reigns of their rulers are the main events that they refer to as time segments. Although most of these people use calendars, there are still many Sotho and Nguni people who speak of time before or after a certain war or ruler. In such cases, the responsibility rests with the interviewer to consult literary sources to date the period referred to by the interviewee.

Independent of their level of literacy, Sotho and Nguni people understand time differently. When referring to a period that has already passed, Zulu people say, '*esikhathini esiphambili*' (in the time before). For them, time comes from behind, passes them and then goes in front (*phambili*). Tswana people will say, '*nako e e tlang*' (in the time to come) because for them the time in question is still to come. For Tswana people, time comes from the front, passes them and then goes behind. Since the understanding of time differs from culture to culture, it is important for interviewers to understand what the interviewees mean when they make reference to time. Ignorance of these conceptions of time may leave oral historians confused and could cause them to miss the meaning of interviewees.

Oral history and gender

Interviewing a man and interviewing a woman are two different things. Ignoring this reality may lead the interview encounter astray. Gender consciousness is a social construct, as David Inglis suggests:

One of the central claims of feminist thought is that biological 'sex' is a separate thing from 'gender' which is a matter of cultural convention. Notions as to which traits 'masculinity' and 'femininity' involve vary from one society to another. What is thought of as 'feminine' behaviour in one context might be seen as more 'masculine' behaviour in another. The fact that a person possesses a certain type of genitals is not enough fully to determine what their behaviour will be like. Instead people conform to the cultural norms as to 'male behaviour' and 'female behaviour' set by the social context in which they live.[16]

Each society constructs its own picture of the differences between a man and a woman and how both are supposed to behave. It is expected that men and women perform different roles in society. Most traditional African societies see men as superior to women, despite women's essential role in matters of production and reproduction.[17] Men are socialised to assume a position of leadership in domestic and public life. As a result, most women in African societies depend on men's favour for survival and make no real attempts to change this social arrangement.

In African societies, men are often reluctant to be interviewed by women on matters of public interest, since traditionally men do not engage with women on such issues. Women, especially if they are not married, are equated to children. When Nokhaya Makiwane, a programme co-ordinator of the Sinomlando Centre, visited a tribal council in the Pietermaritzburg area in the company of a junior male researcher, the elders addressed all their questions to her junior colleague, ignoring her altogether. At times, men find it easier to talk to other men, irrespective of their tribal and racial background. In particular, many African men may not agree to be interviewed if they know that a woman might ask questions about issues such as initiation rites, sexuality and polygamy.

Where a man interviews another man, the interviewee sees himself as occupying a position of importance, as he imparts knowledge to another man. Men perceive women as lacking the ability to keep secrets. This type of gender prejudice is not restricted to traditional African societies. During the apartheid era, Afrikaner men formed a secret society called the Broederbond for men only and the government kept white women in the dark about the atrocities perpetrated by their husbands and sons against black people.

It is important to recognise that not all women willingly accept the patriarchal model. Many South African women, and not only those in urban areas, have developed gender consciousness and resist, directly or indirectly, their fathers', husbands' and sons' dominating tendencies.[18] But, as many oral histories testify, gender oppression has far from disappeared. As a result, many women develop a survivor mentality. They do not want to rock the boat. They recognise the dangers involved in asking difficult questions. They know that they depend on their fathers and husbands as providers. They are socialised to give honour to their male relatives. They tread carefully, lest they endanger the few advantages they have acquired over the years. In an interview, they will often make a point of showing respect to their fathers and husbands. The manner in which these women interviewees address their fathers and husbands shows how much they feel obligated to them. Instead of calling them by their names, they refer to them in the third person – *ubaba wekhaya* (the father of the house) or as the father of their eldest son, *ubaba ka Sipho* (Sipho's father). They may also refer to their husbands by their clan names.

A traditional African woman is not comfortable being interviewed on her own by a man. If her husband is absent, she will often bring along another woman, a neighbour or a friend. There are two reasons for this. First, she has to make it clear to her neighbours and especially her in-laws that she is not involved in an extramarital affair with the male interviewer. Women are often suspected of wanting to have lovers outside of their marriages. Such suspicions are fuelled by the migrant labour system, as Niehaus observed in Bushbuckridge: 'The husband suspects his wife of being unfaithful and does not send remittances, whilst the wife justifies acts of unfaithfulness precisely because she does not receive remittances from her husband.'[19] The other reason for a woman refusing to be interviewed alone is the need to have someone who can witness that the interviewee did not disgrace her in-laws or anybody else, should any sensitive issues be raised. South Africa has a long tradition of suspicion, going back to the days of apartheid when members of the Special Branch wandered around with notebooks and tape recorders.[20]

A person from a culture that holds men and women, young and old, rich and poor in distinct categories may have difficulty relating to an interviewer who does not understand them. Bozzoli writes that older women of Phokeng became anxious and resentful when Mmantho Nkotsoe, the woman who had been interviewing them so far, was replaced by a man who was not even a native Setswana-speaker. They expressed relief when Nkotsoe came back. The fact that she was younger and more educated than them counted less than the shared gender.[21]

The modesty of African women

When interviewed, women rarely feel confident enough to admit that they participated in successful events. Although African men also manifest traits of modesty when talking about their achievements,[22] the habit of understating one's successes is most typical of women. Patriarchal and male-centred societies have inculcated modesty among women such that they may come to believe that they cannot achieve anything without the contribution of husbands, sons or male colleagues. When women step outside of this role, trouble can result. Recently, an acquaintance of mine had an argument with his wife because she had told family friends that she had paid for the two cars owned by the couple. This was the truth, but the husband insisted on creating the impression that he was the main provider of the family.

The Zulu proverb '*indlu yegagu iyanetha*' (the expert's house is prone to leaks) is a reminder that those who boast about their successes also have failures. As soon as a woman sings her own praises, she is dismissed as being too proud. Pride is a sentiment that is frowned upon in traditional African cultures when expressed by women, even though men often unashamedly sing their own praises. At initiation, men are taught to recite with pride their ancestral lineages.[23] These traditions emphasise the achievements of male ancestors, but ignore the contributions of departed women.

For a woman who has never had the opportunity to be interviewed, telling her story can be like discovering a new world. Being interviewed means being recognised as an individual in her own right. To be given the chance to shape the story as she wants to affirms her value and intelligence. The fact that she – not someone else – has been chosen elevates her status in her community. Irrespective of the subject matter of the interview, the interviewee gains importance and develops a new sense of identity.

But for all potential interviewees, especially women, there are also risks. Making themselves available for an interview makes them vulnerable in many ways. They are at risk of being retraumatised when asked to tell about traumatic experiences, for instance, the loss of a loved one. When Cosmos Mzizi, a fieldworker from the Sinomlando Centre, asked women in Bhobhonono, Pietermaritzburg, to share their experiences of the political violence in the late 1980s, they struggled to find words when talking about the deaths of their sons or husbands. This is one way that trauma manifests itself in interviewees' narratives.[24]

Risks of misinterpretation

Because women interviewees tend to feel that they should be modest about their achievements, they face a particular risk of being misrepresented by oral historians. When Katherine Borland, an American feminist writer, showed her grandmother a paper she had written after having interviewed her on her experiences as a woman in the mid-twentieth century, she was told that her paper completely misrepresented the story:

> So your interpretation of the story as a female struggle for
> autonomy within a hostile male environment is entirely YOUR
> interpretation. You've read into the story what you wished to
> – what pleases YOU. That it was never – by any wildest stretch
> of the imagination – the concern of the originator of the
> story makes such an interpretation a definite and complete
> distortion, and in this respect I question its authenticity. The
> story is no longer MY story at all. The skeleton remains, but it
> has become your story. Right? How far is it permissible to go,
> in the name of folklore, and still be honest in respect to the
> original narrative?[25]

An interpretation is not meant to mislead. Because Borland was
interpreting her grandmother's story for a feminist scholarly
readership, her interpretation forged her grandmother's experience
in that image, casting it as a story about resisting male domination.
However, in so doing, she inadvertently silenced her grandmother's
actual intent. Borland's case is a cautionary tale to oral historians to
employ interpretation to make clear the deep currents of the
testimony he or she has collected, not to misinterpret or mislead.

An interview can empower victims of oppression and alienation,[26]
but it can also have the opposite effect. This happens when the
interviewer is so focused on his/her research agenda that he/she
does not allow interviewees to tell their stories as they want to. When
approached for an interview, interviewees start to remember the
events of their lives that they want to share and they plan how they
will tell their stories. They become disillusioned when an interviewer
rigidly sticks to his/her questionnaires and does not give them the
space to tell their stories. Such an experience effectively disempowers
the interviewees. To avoid such a situation in her study of the women
of Phokeng, Bozzoli instructed her fieldworkers to allow interviewees
to guide the interview.[27] In this way, both the interviewee and the
interviewer can be enriched from the interview experience.

The codes of politeness characteristic of African societies can
lead to an impoverishing of interviews if interviewers do not pay

attention to them. Interviewers who correct the language of interviewees or ask them to repeat themselves, as if they were children, induce a sense of discomfort in the interview. To avoid this problem, interviewees may answer in the affirmative to all the questions, an attitude that then leads to poor interviews.

Victims and heroes

As oral historians in South Africa collect the stories of the apartheid era from women and people of colour, themes of oppression and domination are often dominant. However, these themes should not be highlighted to the exclusion of other, more positive dimensions of interviewees' experiences, as this could create a perpetual sense of victimisation. During the apartheid era, the government controlled the past by promoting histories written from the point of view of the dominant culture. The history of black people in general and of women in particular was excluded or distorted. Simply allowing the stories of these people to be told will show that the victims of apartheid cannot simply be described solely as victims.[28]

Kendall, who worked in Lesotho, is one of the writers who moved away from the habit of portraying people as victims. Her storytellers celebrate their success in the midst of chaotic relationships and dysfunctional families:

> The stories also tell about relationships between the sexes in Lesotho: love, marriage, passion, divorce, wife-beating and child-abuse are here, though, in every case, the focus of the story is the decisions women make, the actions they take to protect and to provide for themselves and their children, and in several cases, to care for the women or the men they love. There are no passive victims here, no pitiable characters who are merely haggard survivors of ill fortune. Within the range of choices available to them, these women choose bravely and with conviction.[29]

In post-apartheid South Africa, the government has invested large sums of money, through the Department of Arts and Culture and its provincial equivalents, in promoting oral history.[30] The stories that are brought to the fore celebrate the wisdom and courage of African people and their resistance to apartheid. Cultural expressions through songs, dances and sports are now valued as part of the nation's cultural heritage.

Relatively few oral history projects focus on the survival strategies and resilience mechanisms of the oppressed. As seen above, one of them is Kendall and some of the interviews that she recorded evoke deep emotions. Another example is the work of Haddad, who interviewed Anglican women in Vulindlela, a very poor district on the outskirts of Pietermaritzburg, which also promotes this type of research. Her interviews document 'different aspects of survival in the face of suffering that the women of Vulindlela face'.[31]

'Why me?'

When oral historians approach a potential interviewee, they should always consider what motivates that person to take part in an interview. Kristina Minister, an American oral historian, discusses the contradictory feelings experienced by women when asked to tell their stories. Being interviewed means that one is presumed to have the necessary language skills, but what happens if the person who is interviewed does not see herself as a good speaker?

> Once the purpose of the project is explained, including the standard disclosures and legal agreement, narrators make an accurate inference about one thing that goes in oral history: they are going to display a respectable degree of speaking competence. This supposition contributes to the hesitation of all kinds of narrators to participate. 'All right,' most finally agree, 'but you'll have to ask questions.' What that means is, 'I trust you to guide me through this thing, whatever it is.'[32]

The same applies to interviewees in southern Africa. Why should a person, especially a woman who comes from a disadvantaged background, agree to be interviewed? Is it for fame and fortune? Is it for a special or imagined audience or readership? There are many factors in the willingness to share information, some of which are not divulged to the interviewer. Bozzoli explains why she thinks some women in Phokeng agreed to be interviewed:

> The women who agreed to participate did so for a variety of reasons, each of which leaves its mark on the kind of interview they give. Some agreed because they believed they had an interesting and important story or series of stories to tell. They show a sense of their place in history, and their significance as historical actors. Naomi Setshedi, for example, stops Mmantho and changes the direction of the interview completely at times, with the sense that she knows important things that Mmantho is not particularly good at getting at. Others believe that by participating in the interview some aspect of their lives will perhaps be bettered. One woman refused to be interviewed, claiming that 'nothing had come' of her previous interviews, so why, she asked, should she be interviewed again? Some treat the interview as an occasion to tell Mmantho all the things they have been longing to convey to the younger generation – either about the lost past, their own lost dignity, or about the lost struggles that achieved things which the younger generation now take for granted. The women regard themselves as 'stores of information and history'. They talk about times long ago, and about old practices, sometimes patronising Mmantho with a cultural heritage she 'should' know about, but other times simply telling her that there are things she has not heard of.[33]

The reasons for agreeing to be interviewed, if they have not been expressed from the outset by the interviewees, sometimes become apparent during the interview itself, after the project has been completed or during further analysis when the interview transcripts are scrutinised.

Conclusion: The transforming power of oral history

Haddad observed that Nonhlanhla Magubane, her fieldworker, was transformed by her interaction with the women of Vulindlela:

> She has been challenged to rethink what it means to be an African woman which has been a complex process that carries with it inherent contradictions. On the one side she speaks of learning from the women we worked with that suffering is part of a woman's burden, and says, 'I will still suffer once I have a husband but I will remain strong.' However, on the other hand she asserts that since working with the group she now considers herself a 'feminist'. She suggests that her 'place' as an African woman is to suffer, and yet simultaneously acknowledges that she now recognises that male dominance has 'damaged' and 'disadvantaged' her. These ambivalences and ambiguities suggest the complexity of her reconstitution of identity.[34]

Men and women can become new people after an interview that has some depth. Oral history is an academic discipline aimed at filling in the gaps in historical research, but it is also a human encounter that can have a profound effect on people's lives. It can change the way in which oppressed people, women in particular, see themselves. In the introduction to their anthology, the editors of *Women Writing Africa* make the point that ordinary women can be persons of talent: 'More than corrective, however, the anthology also celebrates women's achievements, voices, and concerns. Our focus is on women's work and thought, through which women may be seen not as passive or barely visible entities, but as articulate and talented producers of art and knowledge, and as heroic makers of history.'[35]

When allowed to tell their stories freely, participants in oral history projects, and even readers of written accounts, can undergo a process of transformation, as they start looking at their own lives, their gender and culture in a different way.

Notes

1. The standard reference on oral history and gender is Sherna Berger Gluck and Daphne Patai, eds., *Women's Words: The Feminist Practice of Oral History* (London: Routledge, 1991). For life stories of women in southern Africa, see Lesley Lawson and Helene Perold, *Working Women: A Portrait of South African Black Women Workers* (Johannesburg: Sached Trust/Ravan Press, 1985); Limakatso A. Kendall, ed., *Basali! Stories by and about Women in Lesotho* (Pietermaritzburg: University of Natal Press, 1995); Beverley Haddad, *African Women's Theologies of Survival: Intersecting Faith, Feminisms, and Development* (Ph.D. dissertation, University of Natal, 2000); Nomboniso Gasa, ed., *Women in South African History: Basus'imbokodo, Bawel'imilambo – They Remove Boulders and Cross Rivers* (Cape Town: HSRC Press, 2006); Amandina Lihamba, Fulata L. Moyo, Mugyabuso M. Mulokozi, Naomi L. Shitemi and Saïda Yahya-Othman, eds., *Women Writing Africa: The Eastern Region* (New York: The Feminist Press, 2007).
2. Albert Luthuli, *Let My People Go* (Glasgow: Collins, 1962), 24.
3. Adam Ashforth, *Witchcraft, Violence, and Democracy in South Africa* (Chicago and London: Chicago University Press, 2005), 68.
4. Philippe Denis, 'Oral History in a Wounded Country', in *Orality, Literacy and Colonialism in Southern Africa*, ed. Jonathan Draper (Pietermaritzburg: Cluster Publications, 2003), 209.
5. Ashforth, *Witchcraft, Violence and Democracy*, 69.
6. For a definition on culture in the African context, see Stuart Bate, *Inculturation and Healing* (Pietermaritzburg: Cluster Publications, 1995); Isabel Phiri and Sarojini Nadar, eds., *African Women, Religion, and Health* (Pietermaritzburg: Cluster Publications, 2006).
7. Isak Niehaus, *Witchcraft, Power and Politics: Exploring the Occult in the South African Lowveld* (London: Pluto Press, 2001), 108–09. In Sotho, an *ngaka* is a traditional healer and *dihlare* are medicines made out of plant or animal products.
8. Axel-Ivar Berglund, *Zulu Thought-Patterns and Symbolism* (Cape Town: David Philip, 1976), 146–47.
9. Kendall, ed., *Basali!*, ix.
10. Belinda Bozzoli, with Mmantho Nkotsoe, *Women of Phokeng: Consciousness, Life Strategy and Migrancy in South Africa, 1900–1983* (London: James Currey, 1991).
11. Haddad, *African Women's Theologies*.
12. Ibid., 28–33.

13. Brian Khoza, 'Crossing the Great Eye Contact Divide', *The Witness*, 30 January 2008.

14. Radikobo Ntsimane, 'Dominant Masculinities within the Zion Christian Church: A Preliminary Investigation', *Journal of Constructive Theology* 12, no. 1 (July 2006): 27–37.

15. Jan Vansina, *Oral Tradition as History* (London: James Currey, 1985), 128.

16. David Inglis, *Culture and Everyday Life* (New York: Routledge, 2005), 31. See also Musimbi Kanyoro, *Introducing Feminist Cultural Hermeneutics: An African Perspective* (London: Sheffield, 2000). 'The fact that gender roles differ significantly from one society to another and from one historical period to another is an indication that they are socially and culturally constructed.'

17. Jeff Guy, 'Gender Oppression in Southern Africa's Precapitalist Societies', in *Women and Gender in Southern Africa to 1945*, ed. Cheryl Walker (Cape Town: David Philip, 1990), 33–47.

18. For an example of women showing signs of gender consciousness in a patriarchal environment, see Philippe Denis, ' "We Also Had to Live with Apartheid in Our Homes: Stories of Women in Sobantu, South Africa', *Studia Historiae Ecclesiasticae* 30, no. 1 (June 2004): 151–67.

19. Niehaus, *Witchcraft, Power and Politics*, 55.

20. Bozzoli, *Women of Phokeng*, 7. See also Manas Buthelezi's testimony on Security Branch harassment in Philippe Denis, Thulani Mlotshwa and George Mukuka, eds., *The Casspir and the Cross: Voices of Black Clergy in the Natal Midlands* (Pietermaritzburg: Cluster Publications, 1999), 60.

21. Bozzoli, *Women of Phokeng*, 10.

22. Nelson Mandela, for example, often says that his personal achievements should be regarded as the result of a collective effort.

23. *Ho ithoka* in Sotho and *izithakazelo* and *izibongo* in Zulu.

24. For more on this issue, see Chapter 7 by Sean Field in this volume.

25. Katherine Borland, ' "That's Not What I Said': Interpretive Conflict in Oral Narrative Research', in *Women's Words*, ed. Gluck and Patai, 70.

26. Denis, 'Oral History', 209.

27. Bozzoli, *Women of Phokeng*, 5, 10.

28. See Chapter 1 by Julia Wells in this volume.

29. Kendall, ed., *Basali!*, xii.

30. Apart from supporting local research projects, some of them based on oral history, the Department of Arts and Culture funds the annual conferences of the Oral History Association of South Africa.

31. Haddad, *African Women's Theologies*, 27.

32. Kristina Minister, 'A Feminist Frame for the Oral History Interview', in *Women's Words*, ed. Gluck and Patai, 28.

33. Bozzoli, *Women of Phokeng*, 11.

34. Ibid., 42.

35. Lihamba et al., *Women Writing Africa*, 1.

6

Are Rural Communities Open Sources of Knowledge?

MXOLISI MCHUNU

COMMUNITY-BASED RESEARCH is becoming popular in the social sciences and humanities. Grant-providing institutions, such as the National Research Foundation (NRF), require collaboration with local stakeholders as a condition of funding scholarly projects in rural South Africa. Some of these communities that play host to researchers are, in turn, insisting on being custodians of oral history and beneficiaries of academic grants. While many oral historians welcome these new developments, they also recognise the difficulties in finding a balance between their research agendas and the expectations of a community that desires to record memories of the past for reasons extending beyond intellectual analysis.

This chapter examines the impact of two oral history projects in rural KwaZulu-Natal on the communities with which these projects partnered. The chapter also assesses the ideas that drove the choice of methodologies in these projects. The first project, my Master's thesis completed in 2005, after nearly three years of fieldwork, explored contested relationships of power among several generations of fathers and sons in rural KwaShange, in the Vulindlela district, near Pietermaritzburg.[1] As the sole researcher, I relied on evidence gathered from the place of my upbringing. Working in my own community, I constantly struggled to maintain adequate objectivity in the interviews and analysis. The insider knowledge of local

129

dynamics that I brought to the interpretation of testimonies both enriched and complicated my work. The second project, an NRF-sponsored study, titled *Impi Yamakhanda* – literally, the 'war of the heads' – reconsidered the legacies of the Bhambatha rebellion of 1906 from an indigenous perspective. I was involved in the fieldwork, which took place in 2004–05 in Engome (Msinga district), a community where I was an outsider. This research tapped into the memories of the *amaZondi* (or Zondi people), whose traditional leader in 1906 was the famous anti-colonial rebel *inkosi* (chief) Bhambatha kaMancinza.

Defining community research and the place of researchers in the community

The ideal of 'community' suggests a harmonious group. In the light of my previous research, I define a community as a geographical area that contains people who share common boundaries, political rules and cultural heritage. However, most communities are not unified; they are fluid social entities, moving between consensus and disagreement. They are also susceptible to rivalries and divided by inequalities. A formulation of 'community' that is focused on unity tends to overlook, for example, how people in rural KwaZulu-Natal have absorbed disruptive historical transformations from migrant labour to apartheid laws. Researchers do better when they identify the ways in which political hierarchies are ruled by *amakhosi* (chiefs) and contested by commoners, and how generational struggles in families guided by *abamnumzane* (homestead heads) influence rituals of patriarchal obedience and gender relations. One important point of discontinuity and contestation within such a community, dealt with in a chapter of my Master's thesis, is the Zulu cultural concept of *ukuhlonipha*, or respect and avoidance, and its very real impacts upon the sexuality of black males. In KwaShange, *ukuhlonipha* stood as a cultural inhibition, dissuading a Zulu father from a discussion about sex with his sons. As an illustration, I found the fact that my family has lived in KwaShange for three generations to be a disadvantage with regard to asking men of my grandfather's generation direct questions concerning their sexuality, as to do so would breach norms of respect governing the interactions of our respective age groups. This very resistance, encountered in the context of research, supports the contention that such cultural norms are, in fact, still highly influential. As a result of these norms, what little sexual education a youth receives comes from younger uncles and peers.

These cultural ideals have repercussions in the public arena as well. An example to indicate how important it is to be sensitive to the cultural value systems of communities under research is Jacob Zuma's rape trial. During this controversial case, many comments were made publicly, including hilarious cartoons showing the irresponsibility of Zuma's failure to use a condom and his statement that showering after sex protected him from HIV infection. As reflected in my research into these matters, I would, as a younger Zulu male, never have been allowed by custom to ask questions regarding an older man's sexuality. For this reason, the rape trial itself, during which the whole country freely discussed Zuma's most intimate behaviour, was an outrage to many of my age, sex and race, as it ran counter to the respect (*ukuhlonipha*) due to Zuma and violated his dignity (*isithunzi*) as a Zulu patriarch and struggle hero and his position as the former deputy-president of South Africa. In this view, the media did not only violate Zuma's privacy, but they also insulted the cultural norms applicable to the interaction between younger men and their fathers. As I see it, it is not the duty of the community researchers to judge a person's actions, but perhaps journalists have another brief. However, as I argued in my thesis, this taboo against speaking of the father's sexuality may well have exacerbated the HIV/AIDS problems of Africa, as youths have sought their information elsewhere and not always from the most responsible or well-informed role models in the community.

As a researcher, I assume that just as I am assessing a community, the community is forming an impression of me. When conducting interviews for my Master's thesis, I sensed that I was evaluated as a young man with familiar ancestral roots and an individual of many parts. KwaShange residents generally accepted me as a son of their traditional community because my father, a man proud of his Mchunu ancestors, lived there and I respected long-standing Zulu customs such as *ilobolo* (bridewealth). My interviewees also knew me as an *ikholwa*, a believer in Jesus Christ, and a member of a charismatic church that prayed in isiZulu, and they kept abreast of my educational advancement as a university student. In addition, like other young men in KwaShange, I was known to walk the path blazed by prior generations, that of a migrant labourer who departed his land-poor reserve for urban opportunity. Indeed, I spent what amounted to only a few weeks a year with my rural family, usually during holidays, spending the rest of my time in Durban, where I worked and studied at the University of KwaZulu-Natal. My experiences, in other words, were as pertinent to my interviewees as their lives were relevant to my research.[2]

Such considerations necessarily complicate how interviewees and researchers construct who is from the community. Researchers should probe the extent to which interviewees embrace multiple community affiliations. This issue is vital to oral historians in determining whether they are known or recognised (i.e. as an isiZulu speaker in an isiZulu-speaking area) or perceived as a stranger.

When researchers try to grasp the differences and similarities between individual and collective identities, it is essential that they avoid assuming too much about interviewees. To expect a person to react in a certain way to an oral history question just because they are of a certain age or gender will often lead to disappointment. Equally apparent to me in KwaShange was that even when interviewees trusted me, some remained wary of university-based written assessments of local realities. Anthropologist Pearl Sithole, a researcher in the *Impi Yamakhanda* project, encountered this response among the Zondi people. She found that writing words down represented 'the arrogance of [official] scholarliness', an intrusive way of knowing in

Engome that evoked memories of colonial authorities with pen, paper and the intent to subjugate Africans with greater effectiveness.[3]

During the *Impi Yamakhanda* field research, when interviewees expressed suspicion of the intentions of scholars, this was based upon previous experiences of academics who had misrepresented data. The *Impi Yamakhanda* researchers gave assurances that the community would be consulted for validation of data, and this later took place in a community workshop before a colloquium in which the writers presented their work in progress. Any resistances expressed by interviewees were noted by the researchers and shared with the *Impi Yamakhanda* committee, and some of these resistances became integral to the study, most notably in 'Freedom Sown in Blood', a chapter written by gender studies academic Thenjiwe Magwaza.

What is the indigenous perspective and why is it important to oral history?

A researcher's awareness of how community identities are formed and how they function will be very helpful to his/her research.[4] More than any other academic discipline, anthropology has contributed the most useful models of African identities. Over the past four decades, anthropologists investigating Zulu 'thought systems', such as Harriet Ngubane, Axel-Ivar Berglund and Absalom Vilakazi have informed oral historians' studies of power relationships in KwaZulu-Natal.[5] Today isiZulu-speaking scholars also embrace Indigenous Knowledge Systems (IKS), an epistemology that brings oral historians and rural communities together in several pursuits, among them recovering pre-colonial and colonial pasts 'of the people and for the people'.[6] The IKS approach has adopted an anthropological emphasis on local fieldwork, but assailed the founding premises of anthropology in South Africa, i.e. the colonial ethnographies condemning 'heathen' habits and government reports tolerating 'tribalism' to uphold white-minority rule, which helped to entrench the racist ideas that culminated in apartheid.[7]

IKS advocates in South Africa draw on the work of pioneering social historians, such as Paul La Hausse, whose scholarship explores

African life during the segregation era in mid-twentieth-century Natal and who supported the liberation struggle in the 1980s from his position as an academic researcher. At the University of the Witwatersrand in Johannesburg, La Hausse and his colleagues Charles van Onselen, Belinda Bozzoli, Philip Bonner, Peter Delius and Santu Mofokeng urged scholars to immerse themselves in an African world of orality. To mark the way, they set out to find and interview the voices of 'history from below'. In so doing, they created a valuable body of testimony generated by black people who not only relayed their resistance narratives, but also told of growing gender and generational struggles within their communities, as colonisers put pressure on families to give up more labour and land to white rulers. Without this interview testimony, La Hausse argues, the perception would remain that most ordinary black South Africans were merely one-dimensional victims of European exploitation.[8]

These historiographical developments informed my graduate research into tensions between fathers and sons in traditionalist families across three generations. These domestic conflicts were exacerbated by a civil war in Natal in the mid-to-late 1980s and early 1990s, which finally abated after the first all-race election led to the dramatic democratic transition in April 1994. During fieldwork in KwaShange, I charted major changes and continuities in Zulu cultural ideals of fatherhood, as they were shaped by recent civil war and 60 years of prior social change under colonialism. The testimonies that I recorded were dominated by the concerns of men of different ages who struggled to fulfil their patriarchal obligations. Interviewees appeared consumed by perceived threats to customary discipline (*inkuliso*) and respect (*ukuhlonipha*). At the height of the pre-election violence, fathers said they could not communicate with sons who continued to protest defiantly against white rule; sons, in turn, claimed their traditionally minded patriarchs did not understand the 'modern aspirations of the new generation'. Such fraying relations stoked political bloodletting, which most journalists attributed to a feud pitting supporters of the non-racial United Democratic Front (UDF) and its African National Congress (ANC) ally against 'Zulu nationalists' in the Inkatha Freedom Party. Contrary to media reports sensationalising tribal rampages between the (Xhosa-headed) UDF/ANC and (all-encompassing Zulu) Inkatha, men in KwaShange said the internecine killings resulted from 'bad blood' between isiZulu-speaking fathers, who felt they were losing patriarchal control, and isiZulu-speaking sons, who 'respected their traditions', but wanted to fight for individual democratic rights.[9] I believe that my status as a researcher, who knew first-hand about filial piety in KwaShange and the local idioms that interviewees used to describe it, enabled me to use oral history to access this deep indigenous perspective.

But exploring indigenous perspectives is not only available to the insider. In fact, there are drawbacks to researchers who are known in a community. In particular, insiders must work harder to maintain objectivity. Other thorny issues may emerge relating to the circulation of interview information. Community members may find it easier to divulge sensitive memories to soon-departing strangers than to veritable neighbours. In this regard, it was instructive to participate in the *Impi Yamakhanda* project, which relied on researchers who were not familiar to Engome residents and, more importantly, subject to local integrity tests before being allowed to enter the community as oral historians. Whatever insider knowledge I could claim, whether linguistic or cultural, was mitigated by the fact that my home was far from where *inkosi* Bhambatha kaMancinza Zondi led the *impi yamakhanda* against a colonial poll tax in 1906. Contrary to my experience in KwaShange, I spent much more time preparing for my research in Engome, learning how to discern Zondi community sensibilities and thinking carefully about what constituted the historical memory of events that occurred in 1906. These challenges were shared by colleagues from different disciplines, who contributed valuable insights.

The *Impi Yamakhanda* fieldwork could only have been achieved by a diverse group of researchers. The collective nature of the intellectual enterprise was enhanced by several workshops led by

Yonah Seleti, then head of the Killie Campbell Library at the University of Natal. He co-ordinated discussions between historians, anthropologists, gender activists, museologists, photographers and graduate students. We debated studies of the 1906 rebellion and combed through relevant archival evidence. Such background sessions would yield methodological breakthroughs, for example, the decision to adopt a life-history approach, and demarcate research parameters, i.e. the sacred topics that were not to be broached in interviews. After reading secondary sources on the cosmological dimensions of the 1906 rebellion, for example, we agreed not to inquire about Bhambatha's grandfather's homestead, a sacred site, or about the stealthy role played by Zondi women who conjured protective magic for their husbands and brothers fighting colonial forces a century ago.

The committee recognised another vital concern, the need to make a formal face-to-face request to the traditional gatekeeper in Engome for permission to enter the community. This appeal was heard by *inkosi* Mbongeleni Zondi, who promptly held *izimbizo* (meetings or debates) with Zondi elders to facilitate the introduction of the university-based oral historians. At the initial *imbizo*, *inkosi* Mbongeleni Zondi presented the names of the researchers and established their credentials, listing among other things their linguistic abilities (the fact that they spoke isiZulu fluently) and their willingness to join communal ceremonies like funerals and work assignments such as cleaning schools. The oral historians who performed these tasks not only learned more about daily life in Engome, but they also fulfilled their obligations as defined by community members. The *izimbizo* deliberations produced another stipulation – namely, that the oral historians owed something to interviewees and their families. *Inkosi* Mbongeleni Zondi decided that his community should benefit by having each oral historian teach research skills to some of the young residents, in the hope that they could use these skills as future tour guides in a battlefield heritage tourism site slated to commemorate *impi yamakhanda*.

My responsibilities entailed collecting *izibongo zikaBhambatha*, the (poetic) praises of Bhambatha Zondi, from *izimbongi*, esteemed praisers.[10] When I recorded the praises, I came across lines such as '*umsongi wensimbi, ayibeke ekhanda*',[11] a phrase alluding to Bhambatha's supernatural strength, his capacity to bend iron into a knot – perhaps a reference illustrating his power to take on a hard enemy, the Natal colonial forces. As with other *izibongo*, Bhambatha's praises were and are performed and reflect the tone and word choice of a spirited praiser. How does an oral historian contend with such shifting oral meanings and indirect explanations? When researchers approach these mysteries of translation, they might take the time to recognise their reliance on indigenous ways of knowing that can contradict long-held 'facts'. For example, in some studies of *impi yamakhanda*, gruesome and controversial legends swirl around Bhambatha's fateful actions in 1906. As books like James Stuart's 1913 *Zulu Rebellion* assert, the Zondi leader of the poll tax uprising was killed in combat at Mome Gorge in Nkandla, with his head later severed by white authorities for identification purposes.[12] Yet Bhambatha's *izibongo* insist that he escaped far north to the Portuguese colonial territory of Mozambique. They also give no year for his death. While this interpretation is certainly debatable, the fact that since 1906, the Zondi people have passed some version of this narrative from generation to generation confirms at least one claim made in Engome: Bhambatha, the fabled hero, lives in popular memory as an icon in South African liberation history.

There is value in recording tales that are difficult to corroborate. Oral historians should strive to gather verifiable evidence, but when they cannot, as in the case of Bhambatha's escape to the north, they should not discount what they have heard. The verses of *izibongo* that chronicled Bhambatha's flight to safety and another life improved my understanding of local political and cultural idioms by illuminating how history is 'intelligently' remembered by the Zondi people. Yonah Seleti's project summary discussed how the IKS focus helped our research team to reconceptualise the 'intelligence' of interviewees:

> [The] western world had really only valued logical, mathemat-
> ical and verbal-linguistic abilities, and had rated people as
> 'intelligent' only if they were adept in these ways. Now people
> recognise the wide diversity of knowledge systems through
> which people make meaning of the world in which they live.
> IKS in the South African context refers to a body of knowledge
> embedded in African philosophical thinking and social
> practices . . .[13]

Such 'social practices' include myths and legends, like the one about Bhambatha's eternity, which revealed how the Zondi people, in my estimation, expressed their will to survive and maintained their resilience in the face of colonial oppression.[14] Researchers entering Engome did not ignore the pertinent publications and archival documentation on *impi yamakhanda*, which drew largely on the writings of colonial observers who disdained African 'intelligence'. Rather, the oral historians assumed that the established literature on the 1906 uprising contained key narratives that would be taken up, confirmed, contested and retold in testimony gathered from Zondi interviewees.

Who controls the indigenous perspective and how should oral historians disseminate it?

Once indigenous perspectives are recorded, oral historians should be aware of an unresolved question that occupies the minds of IKS advocates. Who controls the local knowledge that scholars collect for the purpose of expanding primary sources or publishing copyrighted work? Regardless of how researchers decide to tackle this issue, they should never shrink from the unpredictable exhilaration, ambiguity and ambivalence that come with fieldwork in a rural community. Most importantly, they should honour their interviewees' inherent right to be stakeholders in the research process. In my investigation of generational conflicts, the men I consulted did not question my intentions for doing the research. They expressed interest in my study and requested that their testimonies appear in the text, footnotes and bibliography in order to be known beyond KwaShange. They wanted to have their names included in my Master's thesis because they believed that their testimonies would illustrate how they unflinchingly sought to resolve serious internal struggles.

My pledge to protect the privacy of interviewees was also essential when dealing with families that did not express the above view. Some of these households were seen as provoking discord in the community and bore a stigma that intensified as the HIV/AIDS pandemic decimated parts of KwaShange. With regard to one household, whose seemingly able-bodied members died in quick succession during my fieldwork, rumours spread that the family not only suffered from generational conflict, but also a grandmother who practised witchcraft. She had supposedly killed many people in the past through sorcery. Thus, her adult children were said to be targeted and annihilated by AIDS as a form of retribution for her evil deeds.

The spectre of witchcraft also emerged in the *Impi Yamakhanda* project. There were still strong feelings among the Zondi people about the taboo presence of sorcery in 1906. They maintained, as did some historians, that local *izinyanga* (herbalists) used *intelezi* (traditional medicines) to doctor *inkosi* Bhambatha's *amabutho* (military regiments) in order to make them impregnable to colonial weapons.[15] Thus, researchers were cautioned early on by community members to stay away from one very old Zondi herbalist who was said to possess the secrets of *izinyanga* from 1906. This was once again owing to the taboo nature of this dimension of indigenous knowledge. The old man happened to pass away during the course of the project, and while I regarded his death as a great loss, not least to his family and community and for the wider world that wishes to learn about *impi yamakhanda* from an indigenous perspective, I also appreciated why we could not interview him. The community researchers need to be aware that in traditional thinking (or IKS), explanations with regard to many untoward happenings rest in beliefs in the supernatural. A belief in witchcraft or sorcery is inherent in rural African communities. Once again, the researchers' own religious persuasion must not incline them to dismiss such thinking as mere superstition. Oral historians working in rural KwaZulu-Natal who face some of these challenges should consider the advice offered by Yonah Seleti to researchers in the *Impi Yamakhanda* project: 'The involvement of community members in the production of knowledge' should contribute 'to the promotion of the ownership of intellectual property rights by the communities'. This aim, he adds, 'avoids the monopolisation of knowledge production by the academy [and] takes cognisance of the fact that current intellectual property systems are at odds with the indigenous cultures that emphasise a collective creation and ownership of knowledge'.[16]

Conclusion

How will the new generation of oral historians hear and use testimony in post-apartheid South Africa? Today, the answer may hinge on IKS research and community-based partnerships. Yet we need to be mindful that indigenous knowledge is not without its shortcomings and blind spots, most notably with regard to concerns for issues of gender sensitivity and the allowance of dominant patriarchal explanations. Indeed, there is a contradiction in IKS that allows patriarchy, which is anathema to feminism, and the gender equality entrenched in South Africa's fledgling democracy and its admirable Constitution, which needs to be addressed.

The IKS approach seeks to redress the wrongs of colonialism by giving a voice to African people who were muted, derided as 'unintelligent' and typecast as both ungovernable and exploitable. One of the important outcomes of the *Impi Yamakhanda* project for a researcher like me was that I could tap into pre-colonial values and use these values in ethical oral history research to construct how African people convey the past in idioms that reflect their indigenous culture. By implication, then, my published work, which draws from these indigenous perspectives, will hopefully be valuable in modern South Africa. Unlike prior studies conducted by academics who do not speak an African language, including radical historians, who promoted oral history in the liberation struggle years, my research would be able to reach multiple audiences, those in the world of the university, academia more generally and the stakeholder community itself by means of this old yet new paradigm, the IKS approach.

Yet today, indigenous culture is not something that is unwrapped from a package, having been sealed from colonial influence. What we are tempted to label 'indigenous culture' is a living hybrid, described in isiZulu words such as *isibhamu* and *imoto* ('gun' and 'motor') and metaphors that show how colonial culture was absorbed and made African or Zulu. Perhaps most controversially, indigenous culture in post-apartheid South Africa has a complex place in a new democracy that seeks to uphold the rights of women in patriarchal societies. In particular, I refer to the tension between the parallel legal systems, one called customary law, the other individual human rights. My one experience of the clash between customary law (indigenous perspective) and individual human rights (as enshrined in the South African Constitution) relates to the issue of corporal punishment. Older men as homestead heads had for decades had a customary right or even an obligation to discipline their sons using beatings, yet the new Constitutional law counters this; hence no magistrate will uphold such older customary modes. This is a huge point of contention between the new government and traditional sectors, as the latter, in their anger at seeing their power and control over their sons eroded, readily blame the government and the ANC ruling party, rather than the new culture of human rights. Finally, in this regard, one can return to the point made earlier about communities being subject to internal conflicts, rather than being harmonious unities. To the extent that IKS purports to present something purely and harmoniously indigenous, it may well dishonour its sources, which actually indicate a restless debate on issues of culture.

Notes

1. Mxolisi Mchunu, 'Discipline, Respect and Ethnicity: A Study of the Changing Patterns of Fatherhood of Three Generations of Zulu Fathers and Sons in KwaShange, Inadi, Vulindlela Area of Pietermaritzburg, KwaZulu-Natal, from the 1930s to the 1990s' (Master's thesis, University of KwaZulu-Natal, 2005).

2. In this regard, if an oral history practitioner were to ask me for an interview, he or she would have to learn more about my different identities, starting with the rural-urban divide that defines life opportunities in KwaShange, as elsewhere in rural KwaZulu-Natal.

3. Thenjiwe Magwaza, Yonah Seleti and Mpilo Pearl Sithole, eds., *'Freedom Sown in Blood': Memories of the Impi Yamakhanda, An Indigenous Knowledge Systems Perspective* (Thohoyandou: Ditlou Publishers, 2006), 141. Far from KwaZulu-Natal in Seattle, Washington, a group of mostly white social scientists gauged similar attitudes when conducting oral history research in communities of colour in that American city: Alison Eisinger and Kirsten Senturia, 'Doing Community-Driven Research: A Description of Seattle Partners for Healthy Communities', *Journal of Urban Health* 79, no. 3 (September 2001): 1.

4. Roy Willis, *The Interpretation of Symbolism* (London: Malaby Press, 1975), xi.

5. See Axel-Ivar Berglund, *Zulu Thought-Patterns and Symbolism* (London: Hurst and Co., 1976); A. Vilakazi, *Zulu Transformation: A Study of the Dynamics of Social Change* (Pietermaritzburg: University of Natal Press, 1965).

6. Magwaza, Seleti and Sithole, eds., *'Freedom Sown in Blood'*, 10.

7. For an example of the association between early anthropology, the colonial civilising mission and control of African 'tribal subjects', see James Stuart, *A History of the Zulu Rebellion 1906* (London: Macmillan, 1913). The ethnocentric and racist assumptions upon which this book was based were critically interrogated by the *Impi Yamakhanda* project. See also Mahmood Mamdani, *Citizen and Subject: Contemporary Africa and the Legacy of Late Colonialism* (Princeton, NJ: Princeton University Press, 1996).

8. Paul la Hausse, 'Oral History and South African Historians', *Radical History Review* 46, no. 7 (1990): 346–56. La Hausse acknowledges his intellectual debt to Jan Vansina, *Oral Tradition: A Study in Historical Methodology* (Chicago: Madison, 1985). These form part of the Oral History Programme at the University of the Witwatersrand (Charles van Onselen's African Studies Institute).

9. See Mxolisi Mchunu, '"*Lafa elihla kakhulu*" (Cry Beloved Country): Generational Conflict in the Context of Civil War, in KwaShange, Pietermaritzburg, in 1987–1991', in Mchunu, 'Discipline, Respect and Ethnicity'.

10. Mbongiseni Buthelezi, 'The Empire Talks Back: Challenging the Tyranny of Shaka and Zulu Kingdom Representations in Post-Apartheid KwaZulu-Natal', in *Post Colonialism: South Africa* (Durban: AUETSA, SAVAL and SAACLALS Joint Congress, University of Natal, 2004); Liz Gunner and Mafika Gwala,

eds., *Musho: Zulu Popular Praises* (Johannesburg: Witwatersrand University Press, 1991).

11. Magwaza, Seleti and Sithole, eds., '*Freedom Sown in Blood*', 43.

12. Stuart, *A History*.

13. Magwaza, Seleti and Sithole, eds., '*Freedom Sown in Blood*', 4.

14. Magwaza, Seleti and Sithole, eds., '*Freedom Sown in Blood*', 4; see also Joyce Ladner, ed., *The Death of White Sociology* (New York: Random House, 1973), 38.

15. See, for example, Benedict Carton, *Blood from Your Children: The Colonial Origins of Generational Conflict* (Pietermaritzburg: University of Natal Press, 2000), 134–35.

16. Magwaza, Seleti and Sithole, eds., '*Freedom Sown in Blood*', 10.

7

'What Can I Do When the Interviewee Cries?'

Oral History Strategies for Containment and Regeneration

SEAN FIELD

Introduction

Over the past ten years, I have conducted oral history training workshops with learners, from primary school up to doctoral level, and off-campus workshops with schoolteachers, museum curators and archivists.[1] These learners have encompassed a range of cultural identities with different regional influences, and yet they have repeatedly posed similar questions about oral history practice. One of the most frequently asked questions is: 'What can I do when the interviewee cries?' In most cases, these learners are aware that interviewing can evoke powerful emotions, but they are uncertain how to approach the feelings expressed by interviewees and how to respond to their own emotions. As trainers, we have an ethical responsibility to take these concerns seriously and to try to do more to equip researchers to face these particular challenges of oral history.

In the post-TRC (Truth and Reconciliation Commission) South African context, the common perception that oral history is essentially or only about trauma and related issues is mistaken.[2] In fact, the vast majority of oral history projects do not focus on traumatic experiences and memories. But since the 1960s, oral historians across the globe have focused on 'views from below'; working-class, race, gender and political struggles; human rights abuses; and a variety of community or life histories. It is therefore not surprising that there is a strong likelihood for oral historians to encounter traumatic and/or painful stories during fieldwork. Even if these emotionally laden stories fall outside of researchers' empirical focus, they have an obligation to listen to and reflect on the emotions evoked by their questions and, as far as possible, to contain the interviewee's feelings.[3]

This chapter conceptualises the oral history interview as an inter-subjective dialogue that potentially evokes a wide range of feelings.[4] This conception allows for a clearer understanding of how to develop 'strategies for containment' for memories laden with painful and disruptive emotions.[5] It is the emotions evoked by post-traumatic legacies that most concerns inexperienced *and* experienced oral history interviewers. This chapter suggests guidelines (not rules) for how oral historians might approach interviewing moments that specifically involve interviewees' sadness, pain and trauma. These strategies include attentive listening, sensitive questioning, affirmative mirroring, empathic imagination and being emotionally attuned to the ebbs and flows of the oral history dialogue. There are also guidelines on how oral history interviewers might negotiate their own feelings evoked within and outside of the interview situation. Finally, this chapter argues that by refining these strategies of containment, we can give pragmatic support to the regeneration of people's agency and the resilient ways in which they rebuild their lives after traumatic or painful events.

The oral history dialogue

Although oral historians are not always professional historians, they should bear in mind that the job of the historian is to record, assess and analyse all sources, whether they are constructed through writing, sound, photography or audio-visual techniques. In the selective synthesis and assembly of sources, the historian produces a narrative about the past from a position in the present. But for many oral historians, their primary source is not the interview transcript, or even the audiotape, but the inter-subjective interview dialogue. Oral history is primarily a research methodology. However, if it is only conceived as a means of gathering information, with little or no regard for the subjective nuances of eliciting stories from interviewees, then we do storytellers a serious disservice.[6] From the late 1970s, pioneering oral historians have established the significance of storytelling and the inter-subjective dynamics within oral history dialogues.[7] Alessandro Portelli argues that memory has more to do with the 'creation of meanings' than with what exactly happened in past events.[8] He also points out that so-called mistakes of memory conceal psychological truths, and in approaching these nuances of the oral narration of memories, it is *the dialogue* between interviewer and interviewee that is central.

Yet, in this dialogue, the ignorant person is not the interviewee, but the interviewer. Ignorance or a lack of knowledge about particular research questions is a defining part of our jobs as researchers. It is therefore quite extraordinary how many researchers, especially as they become more experienced, seem to forget this defining feature of research. Retaining an awareness of this ignorance will assist researchers in learning to be humble and respectful when approaching all potential interviewees. It logically follows that oral historians are the ones who are constantly trying to learn from interviewees.[9] The interviewee potentially has the information and knowledge that oral historians need to fulfil their project goals. This is an excellent starting point to learn how to do oral history interviews and to deal with the various challenges of fieldwork situations. In addition, at times – through the dialogue – when interviewers ask insightful questions, interviewees can also learn more about their own lives or see the social and cultural worlds they inhabit in a new way.

Before dealing with the particular challenges of pain and trauma in the oral history dialogue, it is crucial to acknowledge that oral history dialogues evoke feelings for both interviewees and inter-viewers. Oral historians pose questions about various significant themes in an interviewee's life. This means that oral history dialogues have the potential to evoke different feelings, ranging from joy, pleasure, happiness and excitement to fear, anger, shame, guilt and envy. However, researchers often take this emotional range for granted or, instead of defining particular feelings as 'emotions', they refer to them as 'experiences'.

At the beginning of my oral history course, I tell learners that there will be a section on 'emotions and oral history', but learners generally assume that I am *only* referring to pain and sadness. This is linked to a tendency to forge a dichotomy between good feelings, which are taken for granted, and bad feelings, which tend to be their main concern in the research context. I would recommend that researchers need to try to accept all their and interviewees' feelings as legitimate and important. The good and bad feelings distinction increases anxiety and undermines our capacity to deal with the variety of emotions that might be expressed during the interview process.

Taking the interviewees' feelings seriously in an integrated fashion also complements the life-history approach of giving people a space in which they can tell their stories in their own words. While every life story is socially constructed through language, culture and media, how individuals select and splice their memories, which include their feelings, in the interview situation gives us clues to understanding how and why people think and act in the ways they do at different moments in the past.[10] As Anna Green argues, oral historians need to avoid interpreting how narrators understand emotions as passive by-products of social structures or cultural scripts.[11] Rather, if we are to genuinely learn from the interviewee, we have to approach each individual interviewee and interview dialogue as historically distinctive and not with preconceived agendas or paradigms.[12]

The inter-subjective dimension of the oral history dialogue, then, shapes what is said, how it is said and what is not said and is constructed through a complex intersection of the interviewer's and interviewee's identities. Central to understanding this dialogue of identities are degrees of trust and mistrust between interviewer and interviewee. Simply put, would you disclose your intimate stories to someone you do not trust? How we deepen levels of trust is significant to the success of all oral history research practice. While intimate levels of trust are not necessary for all projects, they are essential when conducting projects that require in-depth life stories or evocative projects, such as those that explore topics of conflict, violence and trauma, which will be discussed later. Building trust in the inter-subjective dialogue is initially shaped by establishing research access to the interviewees' stories and then negotiating identity and cultural differences between interviewer and interviewee, which are relevant to the contemporary context of interviewing. For example, in the post-apartheid South African context, a black female interviewee said to me:

> F. D[ike]: So all your life, you are angry and you build a wall inside, that place where if a white person humiliates you, when they hit the wall, you explode. It's something even today that when I look at that wall, it's a wall I can't take down yet because it has protected me for 53 years of my life. I have learned to fight because of that wall. It has been the point for me that when a white person reaches the line, then you tell him off, you tell him where to get off. It has a lot to do with trust. Can I trust a white person to see me as a human being? Then I can lower the wall. Maybe it's like that for white people too? I don't know, but I know every black person has that wall inside. It's like when you had a friend and they've broken your trust, it takes a long time for that to grow back. The person who broke that trust has to work very hard to make up for that. Do you know what I mean?
>
> SF: I know exactly what you mean.
>
> FD: We say white people because the system, that system did it and all the horrors that came with it. Of course, we are still sitting on our sides too scared to bring down the wall.[13]

Acutely aware that I am a white male, the interviewee poses me a test: Was I really listening and understanding her stories? This is a test of the trust between us. It seems that I pass, as she opens up even further and the interview dialogue becomes more relaxed and flowing. In moments like these, it is crucial that interviewers do not take the interviewees' questions personally, but rather accept this as their legitimate right to test whether you are a trustworthy listener of their stories. The profound lesson that the interviewee conveys is that by moving beyond our fears, it is possible to begin to trust each other, but this is a delicate process.

Shared experiences and identities between interviewers and interviewees, such as similar cultural or community backgrounds, can help to facilitate understanding and the building of trust. However, identity or personal differences between the interviewer and interviewee cannot be entirely removed. The common assumption about the oral history dialogue that if all the interviewees' and interviewer's identities are the same, we shall reach an ideal interview situation with no power differences and that 'pure truths' will be discovered is a myth.[14] All oral history dialogues involve a negotiation of various differences of identity. At the very least, there is the fact that we are separate individuals with differing life histories.[15] Yet identity differences need to be approached not as a problem, but as a creative dynamic in the construction of oral histories. The subtle process of eliciting stories from interviewees involves a complex inter-subjective assessment of each other's identities and personalities, and the decisive element to be negotiated in this dialogue is: Can I trust this specific individual with my stories? The negotiation of trust never occurs in a social vacuum, as every oral history dialogue is shaped by a dance between interviewer and interviewee, and evokes a mixture of emotions in both parties. Oral history interviewers need to develop strategies to contain the feelings evoked by their research interventions.

Pain and trauma: Strategies for containment

A broad range of feelings might be evoked within the oral history dialogue, but potentially the most disruptive emotions are pain, hurt and traumatic effects. 'All traumatic experiences are painful. But not all painful experiences are traumatic.'[16] It is important to bear this distinction in mind, as all too often in post-TRC South Africa, many forms of hurt are inaccurately categorised as 'trauma'.[17] Furthermore, a traumatic experience cannot be defined on the basis of the quantity of hurtful experiences felt. A common definition of trauma is that it is an experience or experiences that have specifically ruptured an individual's sense of internal and external realities, and which lead to potential post-traumatic effects, such as numbness, hypersensitivity, nightmares, hysteria, chronic depression, etc.[18] However, trauma is not an external event or contagion that invades or infects a person. Therefore, one person's traumatic experience is not necessarily another person's experience of the same event. Psychoanalytic thinking helps us to understand why particular experience(s) have a traumatic impact on specific individuals, and requires us to consider childhood development and unconscious psychodynamics in understanding different but linked forms of trauma.[19] The emphasis in this chapter is on 'historical trauma' and refers to specific moments in time and space, involving victims and perpetrators, which leave post-traumatic legacies that refer to emotional and material forms of *historical loss*.[20] Moreover, traumatic traces are not only to be found in survivors' internal and emotional selves. In post-apartheid South Africa, this is particularly evident where pre-existing patterns of communicating memories, stories and educational messages across generations, in families and communities, have been ruptured or even destroyed.

Painful and traumatic experiences impact on people's memories and the ways in which they tell their stories and have implications for the interpretation of oral histories.[21] However, interpretation is not the primary focus in this chapter, but rather enabling oral historians to deal with disruptive emotions during the research process. These emotions are not only difficult to confront because of the acute sensitivity involved, but also because traumatic experiences relate to 'limit events', which are beyond the comprehension of both interviewee and interviewer.[22] The traumatic impact of violent events punctures the victim/survivor's pre-existing social, cultural and intellectual forms of comprehension. It is precisely people's frequent inability to understand or explain the events they have experienced, and others' lack of comprehension, explanation or sensitivity, that makes living with post-traumatic legacies so difficult.[23]

Interviewers need to bear in mind how post-traumatic legacies impact on how people remember and narrate their stories. A common example is the repetition of identical stories, in response to different questions. In other examples, interviewees will speak in a monotone, with seemingly no feeling when telling painful stories. In other cases, when interviewees have experienced severe pain, they reach the limits of their vocabulary to describe these memories. At these moments, silences often occur.[24] At times, interviewees will refer to recurring headaches and nightmares at night, which are often traces of trauma. At the limits of linguistic expression or understanding, interviewees also turn to myths, fantasies or forms of magical realism to convey to themselves and the interviewer the painfully indescribable.[25] What strategic skills can oral history interviewers utilise to contain sensitively and respectfully the disruptive emotions that interviewees (re)experience in the oral history dialogue? Bear in mind that these are only brief descriptions of these techniques, which in oral history practice need to be used in an integrated fashion, and are specifically intended for use when interviewing trauma survivors.

Attentive listening

Listening has historically been regarded as the most important skill used by oral historians. Newcomers to oral history frequently think that listening is a simple thing to do, but doing it appropriately and for lengthy interviews of 90 to 120 minutes requires considerable mental energy and the capacity to stay focused on what the interviewee is saying and how they are saying it. In part, the test of a good listener is conveying to an interviewee that you are seriously and attentively listening to their every word. This requires good non-verbal techniques, such as eye contact, calm body posture and nodding the head (not 'ums' and 'ahs').[26] Bear in mind that these techniques have to be appropriately adapted for the particular social and cultural context within which interviews are carried out. When one is unsure of what to do when confronted with painful emotions, the best strategy is to keep on listening.

Emotional attunement

At times, interviewees make their feelings explicit through words, but at other times interviewers need to observe non-verbal cues, such as body language and tone of voice.[27] These techniques are widely used by oral historians, but one additional technique is sensing the mood. The term 'mood' refers to the sense of feelings that exist within the space where the interview dialogue occurs. A sense of mood refers to the inter-subjective framing of the oral history dialogue, which includes unconscious feelings.[28] In this sense, moods are a significant aspect of the inter-subjective dialogue and shape what is being said or not said. The moods of oral history dialogues are often fluid, shifting from anxious beginnings to various moments of joy or pain and sadness. As far as possible, the interviewer needs to try to be aware of what the interviewee is feeling at all times during the dialogue.

Sensitive questioning

The questions prepared by oral historians in planning for the interview and those that are posed spontaneously during the interview must always be sensitive, especially when interviewing trauma survivors. Asking follow-up questions that refer to the stories or content that an interviewee has just presented is a way of showing the interviewee that the interviewer is genuinely listening and interested in what he/ she is saying. Short, simple questions usually work best, irrespective of the educational level of the interviewee. Complex questions or questions that are too long can make interviewees feel as if they are being tested, which is counterproductive to building trust.

How questions are asked is also important, as the speed or tone of voice can either put the interviewee at ease or make him/her feel anxious. When posing questions, an interviewer's voice needs to be calm. Of even greater importance is the timing of questions. Good timing is difficult and relies on the interviewer's intuitive abilities. Sensing the shifting mood(s) of the dialogue is a useful guide to posing specific questions at appropriate moments. Poorly timed questions sometimes do not have an impact, but when interviewing trauma survivors, who may feel emotionally hypersensitive, a mistimed question can be very unsettling for the interviewee. For example, asking potentially sensitive questions about past forms of oppression are best asked when there is a relaxed rapport between interviewee and interviewer.

Affirmative mirroring

It is important that interviewers talk as little as possible during an oral history dialogue, as this is the interviewees' space to tell their stories. Nevertheless, in addition to questions, there are times when it is useful for interviewers to speak. By reflecting back to interviewees that their experiences are interesting, difficult, challenging or reinforcing their own descriptions of events or issues, an interviewer is, in effect, holding up images of the interviewee's self, and in the process his/her sense of self is mirrored. Mirroring is especially crucial in life-story interviewing, as interviewees are often not sure how interviewers are seeing or hearing their stories. It is also a way of building trust in the interview dialogue. However, it is important that these brief words of affirmative mirroring are genuine because interviewees will most likely sense if they are false and this will be counter-productive.

Empathic imagination

Popularly defined, empathy involves 'putting yourself in another person's shoes'. Empathy is not sympathy and it is not a feeling as such, but an act of historical imagination. For oral historians, the research motive is to imagine historically what it was like to be this person, with his/her identity, at a particular point in time and space in the past. Empathy, in one sense, is a visualisation in the interviewer's mind of the interviewee's subjective constructions of his/her memories of experiences. For example, during the 1976 Soweto uprisings, students from Langa in Cape Town also protested and engaged with the police. While reading the following story, imagine the atmosphere and visual setting as the interviewee describes his memories of these violent moments:

> Ja, Xolile was shot in front of what's going to be the museum (i.e. the old pass law office) . . . and if I remember well it is because we were on the march. That was a clean shot just phewww. I remember there was two stories . . . an officer shot him and there was another guy there, police, Mr. Wyngat or something who said, 'I'm giving you two warnings' and he said 'you're not going anywhere' and without a warning shot they shoot him and that's when Xolile fell. We were holding hands like groups of five and he is on there now, this guy was shot on the thigh, he just fell and we caught him. The shot went off from the police and you just see people crumble down and you know he has been hit by a bullet . . . Xolile was a brave man, a brave boy, that's why it was easy for the police to take him because he was a clean target. He was always upfront. A couple of people not only Xolile, was shot in that same incident.[29]

In emotional moments, empathy will help interviewers to affectively connect themselves to interviewees' efforts to express their memories in spoken words, sentences and stories. This empathic strategy allows interviewees more latitude to lead interviewers in new directions, potentially beyond their original research focus. Using empathic imagination requires patient listening to what interviewees want to talk about. By not pushing interviewees to talk within research agendas, interviewers might think beyond their conceptual parameters. This empathic approach helps in eliciting responses from interviewees who have been traumatised, given that their experiences often go beyond the 'limits' of comprehension. Take, for example, this quote from a child survivor of the Rwandan genocide:

> Some days, I think about my mother and my brothers and sisters. Even my grandmother was killed and she was eighty. Thinking about this almost drives me mad and prevents me from studying as I should, especially when I remember a photo of all the members of my family. We had a photo like this in an album which was stolen. This photo often returns to my mind. It reminds me of my dead brothers and sisters, of the way some of them were torn to pieces by grenades. This thought often comes to me during my homework in the evening. Tears follow thoughts like this. After I cry I feel better. I unconsciously find myself reflecting on these things. It's certainly difficult for me to do as well as I should.[30]

As researchers, we will probably never fully comprehend what these experiences felt like, but through empathic imagination, our understanding and interpretations can at least be close approximations. Listening to or even reading stories of such graphic violence is demanding for anyone with feeling and compassion for others. The conventional academic response is to stand completely apart and disinterested from interviewees' emotions. In contrast, Dominick la Capra argues that researchers of trauma need to open themselves to 'empathic unsettlement'.[31] For oral history interviewers, this means that we should not desensitise ourselves to the emotional content of traumatic memories because this will limit our capacity to learn from interviewees. If we are open to our own emotions when we are in the moment of interviewing and empathising with stories of trauma, inevitably we will be unsettled by these emotions. But while 'empathic unsettlement' is a crucial tool, it needs to be counterbalanced by a sense of critical distance from interviewees. Interviewers must maintain personal boundaries or risk the force of the narrators and their own feelings overwhelming them. Simply put, oral historians need to be more emotionally open than conventional academic approaches allow, but they still need to maintain a critical distance from interviewees, out of respect for them *and* in order for research work to take place appropriately.

'What can I do when the interviewee cries?'
The unpredictability of human subjectivity and the fact that interviewees, especially those in marginalised social positions, often experience a feeling of not being heard means that a research interview might trigger emotions. When preparing for an interview, a common interviewer concern, especially for learners, is (even if they know the interviewee): Can I predict and control the emotions that will be evoked in this specific interview dialogue? In short, the answer is no. It is this unpredictability of oral history that makes many interviewers and interviewees feel nervous – or more appropriately, it is called anxiety – in the early stages of a dialogue. In general terms, this anxiety is often about how we might perform in the interview situation or, more specifically, about not knowing whether this interviewee will cry or not. While the vast majority of learners are genuinely interested in learning how to do oral history, this question is usually posed with apprehension and uncertainty.

Sometimes this anxiety is felt because students think that asking about emotions is not academically relevant, as a result of scientific approaches to research, which exclude human emotions and subjectivity. Sometimes this anxiety is evoked because listening to other people's sadness, pain and related emotions is an understandably difficult challenge to face. Sometimes this anxiety is evoked because the prospect of negotiating these intense emotions on your own as an interviewer, especially if you are a young interviewer listening to the anguish of an older storyteller, is a scary prospect. On the one hand, I would recommend that interviewers acknowledge these anxious feelings as legitimate and that they try not to be self-critical for feeling this way. On the other hand, interviewers also need to work at ways to not allow their anxiety to be visible to interviewees. Our anxieties can make it more difficult for interviewees to feel at ease. Often the best way to practise keeping your own anxieties contained within you is by doing practice interviews with friends and, of course, the actual experience of doing more and more oral history interviews is the best learning experience. The main advantage that young interviewers have when working with older interviewees is that interviewees are more likely to be considerate and patient with learners who are learning the skills of their trade. However, over time, all interviewers need to aim to develop a calm and humble confidence to listen to whatever interviewees express.

Guidelines

The following suggested responses to the central question of this chapter need to be adapted to the specific research contexts faced by individual researchers. There is no perfect formula, but these guidelines have a reasonably high degree of success in interviewing moments where sadness is evoked. If interviewees show signs of crying, but continue talking, it is best for interviewers to keep listening and to stay attuned to their emotions. Interrupting or changing the topic at this moment is very inappropriate. When an interviewee stops talking and there is a natural pause, it is imperative that an interviewer should do two things. First, sensitively acknowledge the interviewee's sadness and/or tears. Simple words, such as 'I notice you have been crying or had tears in your eyes while telling that story', are most effective. Second, the interviewer should offer the interviewee the option to pause or temporarily withdraw from the interview. Immediately after acknowledging their sadness, suggest this offer, but it must be the interviewee who chooses what happens next. At such moments, interviewees usually regain some sense of control, although their feelings probably are being experienced as out of control. In my experience, interviewees usually opt to continue or to take a few minutes to compose themselves by getting a tissue or going to the toilet. Through sensitive acknowledgement, the interviewer is also aiming to validate the positive value of crying and simultaneously containing these emotions within the interview space defined by their dialogue.

If interviewees remain unsettled or tearful after an interview is over, it is helpful for the interviewer to remain behind to listen to their stories. While it is not our job to 'cure' interviewees, we do need to take responsibility for the fact that our interview questions and interventions have evoked memories that are laden with particular emotions. If the interviewer is operating in an ethical and sensitive manner, by raising our questions, we are providing a safe space for these emotions that are beneath the surface to be expressed openly. It is at such moments of vulnerability when sadness surfaces that the interviewee is consciously or unconsciously beginning to trust the interviewer. Suggesting psychotherapy is sometimes appropriate, but this must be carefully articulated to avoid making the interviewee feel stigmatised as 'mentally ill', a common misperception of psychotherapy in many communities. At the very least, interviewees can be encouraged to draw on the support of family, friends, elders or respected people in the community, such as priests, doctors or teachers.

Ultimately, there are no guarantees in dealing with people's emotions, but if we display the emotional strength to bear what are often unbearable emotions for the interviewee, we are doing a profound and possibly immeasurably helpful task. However, oral historians must be realistic in what we promise interviewees at all times in the process and we should not portray ourselves as having power to remove people's pain and trauma. We must also be realistic in our own expectations of what is possible in an oral history dialogue. If we have grandiose fantasies of what oral history is capable of, we are setting up ourselves and oral history methodology for repeated failures. In my experience, most oral historians have an understandably altruistic desire to help others in pain, but we must not promise either explicitly or implicitly more than we can deliver. In fact, even trained psychotherapists cannot entirely remove the pain attached to traumatic events of the past. To some degree, post-traumatic legacies always leave emotional remains in the memories of trauma survivors. For example, here is another story of a survivor from the Rwandan genocide:

> I always see the ruins of our house. I see Tutsi neighbours who had children of my age and whose families were wiped out. I live in eternal pain. I saw terrible things. I had never seen a dead person before. I was frightened of dead bodies. Even when my grandmother died, before the genocide, I refused to see her body. But during the genocide I saw lots of dead bodies and people in agony. This will never be wiped from my memory. When I sleep at night and dream, these images come back to me and frighten me. I also dream about the militia chasing me, in order to kill me.[32]

In emotional moments, oral history interviewing resembles psychotherapy.[33] Both oral historians and psychotherapists share an emphasis on the importance of attentive listening and empathy. It is quite clear that oral historians can learn much from the experiences of psychotherapists, but it is essential to understand that we are researchers recording and analysing information and are not trained to attend to psychological problems, as are counsellors and psychotherapists.[34] The oral historian's interaction with interviewees is often only one or a few sessions, whereas for therapists, especially in long-term psychotherapy, the person has contracted to work with the therapist over several months and often years. The oral historian's approach to questioning tends to be more directed, whereas in psychoanalytic practice, the analyst reflects back the emotional content of the person's words. While there are differing approaches, over the past three decades, many in both professions have placed emphasis on interpreting the inter-subjective dimension of dialogues and on 'learning from' the patient or narrator.[35]

'What can I do when I feel like crying in the interview?'

From the beginning of the research process, researchers need to know that there are safe spaces outside the interview space for them to express their emotions or to be debriefed by a supervisor or counsellor.[36] However, during exchanges with interviewees, interviewers need to maintain a gentle calmness, which means, as far as possible, they cannot express their emotions. In short, as much as the hurt and sadness of interviewees might evoke such emotions in oral historians, we should not cry during an interview. Learners and even experienced oral historians sometimes find this a difficult point to accept. Even though we are an important part of the construction of the dialogue, the oral history interview is the interviewees' space to express their stories and emotions, not ours. If we cry, it might distract interviewees from dealing with their complex emotions. The interviewees might be drawn to comforting us, when it is we who should be containing their emotions. Most significantly of all, if we cry, interviewees might consciously or unconsciously perceive their own emotions as unbearable to us, which then directly contradicts our responsibility to bear witness to their emotionally laden stories. If interviewers are struggling with their feelings during an interview, they should establish an internal mental dialogue with their emotions, aimed at delaying, rather than denying, these emotions. If this fails, they need to reflect on their feelings and why they could not contain themselves within a specific interview.

Sometimes, after doing many interviews with trauma survivors, there is a risk of interviewer burn-out. This may be reflected in moodiness, an inability to stay focused, depression and suicidal fantasies. Therefore, it is crucial that after leaving an interview situation, we must not bottle our feelings inside, but rather find ways to express our emotions through talking to someone, such as a therapist, partner, family member, friend or emotional confidant. At the very least, interviewers can write out their emotions in a diary. In South Africa, the TRC itself and non-governmental organisations (NGOs), such as the Trauma Centre for Survivors of Violence and Torture, are aware of these risks, but this is less evident among university researchers.

In teaching situations at schools, colleges and universities, it is imperative that teachers and research supervisors see their role as including listening to the post-interview emotions of their learners. While teachers and lecturers are not therapists, we have an ethical responsibility to listen sensitively to the post-interview emotions and issues that learners express. Furthermore, learners themselves can develop support networks or mentoring roles with senior students to help each other through the emotional challenges of doing oral history fieldwork.

As a general rule, I would argue that it is essential for oral historians and related qualitative research interviewers who do work on traumatic and painful subjects to develop their capacity to be self-reflexive. The more we understand, in the first instance, what motivates us to do this kind of research, the better we will be at containing both our own and others' emotions. We need to continually reflect on and work through our emotions and emotional investment in oral history work. Denying your feelings or pretending to be strong will undermine your capacity to approach interviews with sensitivity and openness. The more open interviewees sense you are, the more they are likely to trust you and disclose their memories and stories. Moreover, by taking inter-subjectivity seriously, our research findings will potentially become more objective, not less, and, simultaneously, we avoid the myth of our own 'objectivity' as being free of human subjectivity and values.[37]

Oral history and regeneration[38]

If oral history researchers are neither therapists nor healers, how can we help interviewees? It logically follows from what I have argued so far that by providing safe spaces for interviewees to convey their memories and stories, with all the emotions they wish to express, we are beginning to help interviewees process the emotional impact of their past experiences. Furthermore, through the specific strategies of containment outlined above, oral historians are helping interviewees in subtle ways to make their unbearable emotions become more bearable. To put it differently, by providing a narrative space to bear witness, oral historians cannot cure or take away interviewees' pain and suffering, but telling their stories *might* make the emotional burden of post-traumatic legacies less difficult to live with. These ways of coping with emotions can also contribute to people shifting from being victims to survivors. While trauma survivors are usually victims of past abuses, oral historians should not exaggerate the victim dimension. This tendency can also be avoided by respecting the resilient ways in which people do interpret, cope with and rebuild their lives after potentially shattering past events. Moreover, if oral historians can contribute to trauma survivors' well-being by acknowledging that they are not sick or bad for feeling what they are feeling and that they are not alone in their suffering, these are useful contributions. In this specific respect, the other significant area in which oral historians can make contributions is through the popular dissemination of people's stories.

While it has appealed to generations of oral historians, the rhetorical idea of 'giving a voice to the voiceless' is misleading and reinforces the idea of 'victims'. Rather, I argue that ordinary people do tell their stories and express their issues, but the problem more accurately framed is as follows: Is anyone listening? Marginalised or traumatised people frequently have insufficiently enabled public voices because of a lack of resources and access to media and empathic listeners. In the South African context, it is still common practice for the post-interview participation of interviewees to be reduced to brief consultations. It is especially at universities that oral historians usually retain the power to shape and voice historical knowledge. In part, this is due to our failure to change institutionalised knowledge/power relations and, in part, it is attributable to the fragile political and financial location of most oral historians.[39] I think that South African oral historians can learn a lot from participatory research methodologies, where interviewees are actively involved as co-creators of the public outcomes of oral history projects.[40]

Oral historians can forge public spaces where people talk, write, perform and represent their memories. However, interviewees need to be forewarned that the public reception of their stories can be a bruising encounter, where 'the work of bearing witness is constantly involved in the struggle against collective indifference and the forging of solidarity between eyewitnesses and audiences'.[41] The multimedia and multilingual dissemination of oral histories through books, radio, film documentaries and the Internet increases possibilities for mirroring both individuals and communities. For the potential of oral history methods to be harnessed, they need to be combined with strategies to build accessible archives, museums, memorial sites, school training and urban or rural renewal projects. For example, the Centre for Popular Memory – a university-based oral history unit – has utilised travelling exhibitions as a useful dissemination tool.[42] These exhibits combine audio, photographs and audio-visual means to tell people others' stories in an accessible fashion. These exhibits are digitally printed on fabric, which are easily rolled up and transported to schools, museums and NGOs in various communities. The audio or audio-visual stories on CD or DVD accompany these travelling exhibits.

These dissemination strategies create opportunities for people with shared experiences and memories to make meaningful connections with each other. The Kulumani organisation developed during and after the TRC is a prime example of how trauma survivors supported each other and advocated for greater support from government structures.[43] Through recording and disseminating oral histories, we can help people to identify the social interconnectedness of past experiences and current memories. These moments of social identification create possibilities where marginalised people *might* regenerate themselves.

Regeneration can be traced in the resilient ways that people work through the 'effects of trauma by generating counter forces' and which potentially motivates their sense of agency.[44] It involves people's own efforts to emotionally revitalise their lives. However, for most survivors, life will not be restored to what it was before the traumatic events of the past. For many, the focus of regenerative activities is to build across generations through parenting and storytelling within families, schools and communities. In this regard, the emergence of community museums draws heavily from oral history recordings and dissemination, which encourage community participation and the possibility for previously dislocated communities to regenerate themselves as a collective entity and identity. Another regenerative process is the growing use of oral history in conjunction with the memory-box technique with people living with HIV/AIDS in various projects across South Africa.[45] However, given poverty levels in South Africa, the age of many survivors of apartheid traumas and the fact that many will have untimely deaths due to various diseases, regeneration is often about creating less painful conditions of life for their children.

Regeneration as a collective process, as described above, or as an individual narrative working through emotions can help people to rebuild their lives, but it 'does not mean total redemption of the past or healing its traumatic wounds'.[46] The emotional and social legacies of trauma remain, but through regeneration, survivors can cope better with these legacies and sustain their resilience and a more confident sense of agency. The potential role of the oral historian is not as healer, but as facilitator. Regenerative memory work is also not about putting the past to rest, but it is about sensitively disseminating contested views of the past. This means not simply adding oral histories to fill in the gaps of national archives or academic historical accounts, but giving narrators greater opportunities to hear and see their stories represented and performed in public spaces. In the process, narrators and various audiences can be stimulated to think about and debate issues and not be treated as passive recipients.

Through these public representations, dialogue will be stimulated in which people can debate local and national versions of South African histories for themselves. This might also involve discussions over whether or not post-apartheid healing and reconciliation has worked at various sites across the country. The past is not fixed, but is contested through narration, dissemination and public reception in the present. By assisting people who have been hurt and traumatised to exercise their right to tell their stories to many audiences, oral historians are making contributions to social regeneration.

Conclusion

This chapter is a response to the legitimate concerns of learners. Unfortunately there is no way for any teacher to completely remove these concerns about dealing with disruptive feelings of pain, sadness and trauma that may be evoked during an oral history dialogue. However, there are dynamic strategies of containment that can be adapted for different research contexts and that can facilitate a more trusting and meaningful oral history dialogue for both interviewers and interviewees. Each new interview potentially poses new challenges, which makes oral history practice both an anxious and exciting experience. It is rewarding to witness people move from moments of pain and sadness – experience some emotional release – and then for them to see their past and present lives with new insights. These insights can help, but for regeneration to be sustained, individuals need the ongoing support of others in their families, communities and other collective networks. In this regard, the popular dissemination of oral histories can help to stimulate links and regenerate emotional connections between people who previously suffered on their own. These are small but profound contributions that oral historians can make to a more bearable future for others who continue to suffer.

Notes

1. I have conducted workshops at the universities of Cape Town, Western Cape, Rhodes, Mauritius, Philippines, and Vietnam. Off-campus workshops were held at the Robben Island Museum, South End Museum, Sol Plaatje Museum, Western Cape Provincial Museums Services, State Archives, Department of Education and South African Democratic Education Trust.
2. Many thanks to the anonymous reviewer for making this point.
3. See the appendix to Alistair Thomson, *Anzac Memories: Living with the Legend* (Melbourne: Oxford University Press, 1994).
4. There are several references to inter-subjectivity in Robert Perks and Alistair Thomson, eds., *The Oral History Reader*, 2nd ed. (London: Routledge, 2006), especially the chapter by Valerie Yow, ' "Do I Like Them Too Much?" Effects of the Oral History Interview on the Interviewer and Vice Versa'.
5. 'Strategies for containment', in the oral history context, refers to interviewees composing narratives that will help them to better understand and to feel more composed with their feelings, within themselves and as expressed to others. For more details, see the methodology section in Thomson, *Anzac Memories*.
6. Kathryn Anderson and Dana C. Jack, 'Learning to Listen: Interviewing Techniques and Analyses', in *Women's Words: The Feminist Practice of Oral History*, ed. Sherna Berger Gluck and Daphne Patai (New York: Routledge, 1991), 11–26.
7. Alessandro Portelli, *The Battle of Valle Giulia: Oral History and the Art of Dialogue* (Madison: University of Wisconsin Press, 1997).
8. Alessandro Portelli, *The Death of Luigi Trastulli and Other Stories: Form and Meaning in Oral History* (Albany: State University of New York Press, 1991), 52.
9. For African examples, see Luise White, Stephan Miescher and David Cohen, eds., *African Words, African Voices: Critical Practices in Oral History* (Bloomington: Indiana University Press, 2001).
10. Sean Field, 'Remembering Experience, Interpreting Memory, Life Stories from Windermere', *African Studies* 60, no. 1 (2001): 131.
11. Anna Green, 'Individual Remembering and "Collective Memory": Theoretical Presuppositions and Contemporary Debates', *Oral History* 32, no. 2 (2004): 35–44.
12. Anderson and Jack, 'Learning to Listen', 12.
13. Interview with Ms. F. Dike by Sean Field, Cape Town, 24 April 2002.
14. Kum Kum Bhavnani, 'What's Power Got to Do with it? Empowerment and Social Research', in *Deconstructing Social Psychology*, ed. Ian Parker and John Shotter (New York: Routledge, 1991).
15. Portelli, *The Death of Luigi*, 31.
16. Sean Field, 'Beyond "Healing": Trauma, Oral History and Regeneration', *Oral History* 34, no. 1 (2006): 31–42.
17. The Truth and Reconciliation Commission (TRC) was a national response to

'horrendous human rights abuses' committed between 1960 and 1994, through documentary investigation and oral testimonies. See Deborah Posel and Graeme Simpson, eds., *Commissioning the Past: Understanding South Africa's Truth and Reconciliation Commission* (Johannesburg: Witwatersrand University Press, 2002).

18. Kim Lacy Rogers, Selma Leydesdorff and Graham Dawson, eds., *Trauma and Life Stories: International Perspectives* (London: Routledge, 1999).

19. Dominick la Capra, *Writing History, Writing Trauma* (Baltimore: Johns Hopkins University Press, 2001).

20. Ibid., 42. Bear in mind this chapter focuses on victims and survivors and not on the challenges of interviewing perpetrators. See Pumla Gobodo-Madikizela, *A Human Being Died that Night: A Story of Forgiveness* (Cape Town: David Philip, 2003).

21. Daniel Reisberg and Paula Hertel, eds., *Memory and Emotion* (Oxford: Oxford University Press, 2004).

22. La Capra, *Writing History*, 1–43.

23. See, for example, a discussion of the link between intelligence and resilience in Richard McNally, *Remembering Trauma* (Cambridge, MA: Belknap Press/ Harvard University Press, 2003), 92.

24. Shosana Felman and Dori Laub, *Testimony: Crises of Witnessing in Literature, Psychoanalysis and History* (London: Routledge, 1992).

25. Alessandro Portelli, 'Uchronic Dreams: Working Class Memory and Possible Worlds', in *The Myths We Live By*, ed. Raphael Samuel and Paul Thompson (London: Routledge, 1990).

26. 'Ums' and 'ahs' expressed while the interviewee is speaking is a technical problem because it often blocks out the recording of their words.

27. Paul Thompson, *The Voice of the Past: Oral History*, 3rd ed. (New York: Oxford University Press, 2000).

28. Robert Stolorow, 'An Intersubjective View of Self Psychology', *Psychoanalytic Dialogues* 5, no. 3 (1995): 393–99.

29. Interview with M. Mtshula by Sean Field, Cape Town, 5 May 2002.

30. African Rights (Kigali, Rwanda), *A Wounded Generation: The Children Who Survived Rwanda's Genocide*, discussion paper, no. 14 (2006), 5 (accessed via e-mail). See http://www.africanrights.org, accessed 27 May 2008.

31. Dominick la Capra, *History and Memory after Auschwitz* (Ithaca: Cornell University Press, 1998).

32. African Rights, *A Wounded Generation*, 11.

33. For a useful comparison of psychoanalytic and oral history techniques, see David Jones, 'Distressing Histories and Unhappy Interviewing', *Oral History* 26, no. 2 (1998), 49–56.

34. Michael Roper, 'Analysing the Analysed: Transference and Counter-Transference in the Oral History Encounter', *Oral History* 31, no. 2 (2003): 20–32.

35. Patrick Casement, *On Learning from the Patient* (London: Tavistock Publications, 1985).

36. Many thanks to Philippe Denis for stressing this point and for other useful comments on this chapter.

37. Yow, 'Do I Like Them Too Much?', 63.

38. Several paragraphs in this section are drawn from Field, 'Beyond "Healing"', which provides a detailed exposition of the regeneration argument in relation to oral history.

39. The proliferation of South African oral history projects and the establishment of the Oral History Association of South Africa (OHASA) in 2005 will hopefully increase awareness around issues of post-interview participation of interviewees and ethics.

40. Note the admirable work of Kirsten Folke Harrits and Ditte Scharnberg, 'We Ourselves are History: An Oral History Project in Denmark', in *Proceedings of the 12th IOHA Conference, Pietermaritzburg, 24–27 June 2002* (Pietermaritzburg: Sinomlando Centre, 2002), Vol. 3: 1100–115.

41. Fuyuki Kurasawa, 'A Message in a Bottle: Bearing Witness as a Mode of Ethico-Political Practice'. http://research.yale.edu/ccs/papers/kurasawa_witnessing.pdf, accessed 1 February 2005.

42. The Centre for Popular Memory trains learners in oral history methodology and conducts research projects on various topics, such as apartheid forced removals, popular culture and refugees, trauma and memory studies. The Centre also disseminates oral histories through books, radio and film documentaries and it has developed an online, fully searchable database: http://www.popularmemory.org.za, accessed 27 May 2007.

43. Kulumani is a non-governmental organisation (NGO) with a network of branches across South Africa providing material and psychological support to victims of apartheid violence. It also has an advocacy function, which involves ongoing work on apartheid reparation and justice issues.

44. Dominick la Capra, *History in Transit: Experience, Identity, Critical Theory* (Ithaca: Cornell University Press, 2004), 119. For example, see Pat Barker, *Regeneration* (London: Penguin Books, 1991). Note that I am *not* referring to the 'moral regeneration movement' in South Africa.

45. Philippe Denis, ed., *Never Too Small to Remember: Memory Work and Resilience in the Times of AIDS* (Pietermaritzburg: Cluster Publications, 2005).

46. La Capra, *History in Transit*, 119.

Appendix 1

Checklist for Oral History Projects[1]

Preparation stage

1. Select a topic and formulate broad questions.
2. Conduct background research for the topic.
3. Develop interview questions.
4. Gain ethical clearance (e.g. from academic institutions, government or local authorities).
5. Identify potential interviewees.
   a) Make initial contact (by phone, or in some cases, in person) to determine if a potential interviewee has experiences relevant to the topic.
   b) Inform the interviewee of the purpose of the interview.
   c) Inform the interviewee that he/she will be requested to sign a consent form.
6. Consider funding needs.
7. Obtain equipment and gain familiarity with its operation.

Production stage

8. Schedule interview(s).
9. Finalise logistical details (transportation, translator, etc.).
10. Get consent form signed by the interviewee.
11. Conduct interview.
12. If photographs are obtained, get photo permission form signed by the interviewee. Provide receipt for any material borrowed from the interviewee.

Post-production stage

13. Transcribe interview.
14. Proofread interview and make corrections.
15. Send hard copy of transcript to the interviewee for correction (spelling of names, places, etc.).
16. Edit transcript; print final copy.
17. Consolidate findings (i.e. in thesis, article, book, pamphlet).
18. Label tape and disc with name and address of the interviewee, date of interview, and type of software of file. Place in archive.
19. If photographs or other materials have been borrowed from the interviewee, duplicate the originals and place in archive. Return originals to the interviewee.
20. Ensure appropriate care and storage of original recordings. Duplicate originals to new preservation media before the original technology becomes obsolete and inaccessible.
21. Give a copy of the transcript and tape to the interviewee. You may also give works created from the oral history material (thesis, book, etc.). Ensure that the portions of the material allowed under the terms of the release document are available and accessible to the community that participated in the project.
22. Wrap-up (e.g. written letter of thanks to the interviewee; witness session; etc.).

Note

1. Compiled by Benedict Carton and Louise Vis. The 'Oral History Checklist' used by the University of Texas was used as a template. See http://www. texan.cultures.utsa.edu/memories/TEXT/pdfs/OralHistoryChecklistFor Interviews1.pdf, accessed 7 July 2006.

Appendix 2

Code of Ethics for Oral History Practitioners in South Africa[1]

When planning an oral history project

1. Consider any possible harm that the interview process may cause to the interviewee's feelings or reputation or to his/her community.
2. Acquire sufficient technical knowledge to conduct an interview of the best possible standard.
3. Obtain the best possible knowledge on the culture and habits of the interviewee and his/her community.

Before the interview

4. Follow a culturally appropriate protocol when approaching the interviewee and requesting an interview.
5. Inform the interviewee of the purpose of the interview, ensuring that he/she has understood this.
6. Agree on the place, time and circumstances of the interview.
7. Agree on whether or not the interview should remain confidential and on where and how the interview material will be stored and disseminated. This should be done in writing (release form) or verbally, with a record on tape.
8. Agree on how the interviewee will benefit from the interview (e.g. receiving a copy of the tape and transcript or a community celebration). Ensure that interviewees do not have false expectations.

During the interview

9. Respect the interviewee's style of personal interaction (language, posture, dress, eye contact, etc.).
10. Be gender sensitive.
11. Deal appropriately with painful and emotional issues.
12. Verify that the interviewee remains comfortable with the interview process and, when necessary, grant him/her the right to withdraw.

When processing the interview

13. Ensure that the interview is transcribed, indexed, catalogued and made available as agreed with the interviewee.
14. Ensure that all possible measures are taken to preserve the interview material.
15. Inform the interviewee of any change regarding the storage or dissemination of the interview.
16. Verify that no part of the interview has defamatory content.

On completion of the project

17. Report back to the interviewee or his/her community and give them a copy of the recording, if an undertaking to do so has been given.
18. Acknowledge the contribution of the interviewee and his/her community in any form of subsequent publication.
19. Share with the interviewee or his/her community any form of financial benefit that may accrue to the interviewer (where applicable).

Note

1. This code of ethics was adopted by the Oral History Association of South Africa (OHASA) at its fourth annual conference in Polokwane, 23–26 October 2007. See http://www.ohasa.org.za, accessed 20 May 2008.

Appendix 3

Interview Release Form[1]

This agreement ensures that your interview is added to the archived collections of _______________________________ (*institution name*) in accordance with your wishes.

I, _______________________________ (*interviewee's name*), hereby authorise _______________________________ (*interviewer's name*) to record my name, likeness, image and voice on tape, film or otherwise to be used in the archived collections of the _______________________________ (*institution name*).

In consideration of my participation in said recording, I agree that:

- The 'original' recording will be conserved at the _______________________________ (*state archival location*). Copies will be held and made available as a public reference resource for possible use in research, teaching, publication, electronic media (such as the Internet or the World Wide Web) and broadcasting (such as radio or television). Copies may be made available, in whole or in part, in any and all media, in perpetuity, throughout the world, subject to limitations stated below.
- All public use is made in strict accordance with the uses and restrictions mentioned below.
- All public use is made in strict accordance with copyright law and 'fair use' provisions.
- The _______________________________ (*institution name*)

shall hold the copyright in this recording and I hereby cede any copyright that I may have in my contribution to it.

- Any and all revenue acquired from this recording will be used to subsidise future research and archival projects of the ___________ _____________________ (*institution name*).
- This agreement represents the entire understanding of the parties and may not be amended, unless agreed to by both parties in writing.

The use of the recording is subject to the following restrictions (where appropriate):

1. I require my name to be kept confidential and anonymity to be preserved.
   YES/NO ________________
2. Other restrictions

____
____
____

Interviewee's signature _______________________________________
Signed at ____
*Date*_______________________________________
Interviewer's signature _______________________________________

Note

1. Adapted from the form used by the Centre for Popular Memory, Department of Historical Studies, University of Cape Town. http://www.popularmemory. org.za/docs/CRform.doc, accessed 20 May 2008.

Appendix 4

Example of a Structured Interview[1]

Do you know who the paternal ancestor (white male) of your family was?
No.

What relation are you of this person? Was he your father, grandfather or great-grandfather?
He was nothing to me.

Do you know if the above-mentioned ancestor had a coloured or black wife?
He was having a black wife.

If she was a black lady, do you know which ethnic group she is from?
She was Pulana.

When they married, did they live together, or did he (your paternal ancestor) live apart from the family?
Staying together.

Do you know of any white men who lived in the area who had more than one wife (one legal and one common-law wife)?
No.

Did your paternal ancestor acknowledge his coloured children (publicly or privately) or not?
Publicly.

Note

1. Extract: Pilgrim's Rest Museum, Treasure Project Questionnaire, 1999. Selected by Cynthia Kros and Nicole Ulrich.

Appendix 5

Guidelines for Oral History Projects in Schools[1]

1. Educators need to make sure that their learners are thoroughly prepared before they go out for an interview. Proper research should be done beforehand.

2. The learner should make an appointment with the interviewee. The learner should explain what the interview is about. The learner should know as much as possible about the interviewee's culture and preferred language/s.

3. The learner should have an idea about what questions to ask. Close-ended questions are usually not good for an interview because they direct the interviewee what to say. Learners should ask uncomplicated questions. Questions should be clearly phrased. Teachers should help the learners to think about the areas that the interview will cover – family, early life and so on.

4. Learners should always be punctual and polite; ask permission to use equipment like tape recorders and cameras; ask the interviewees whether it is acceptable to use their names or if they would prefer pseudonyms; show respect and not interrupt; not force interviewees to answer questions they don't want to; remember they are the interviewers and therefore should speak less than the interviewee; ask if there any materials to support the interview, for example, photos or letters. They should return these materials.

5. Learners should not make any promises to interviewees that they can't keep.

6. Educators should help learners learn to check their equipment

before the interview; to have spare batteries and tapes; to mark the tapes correctly.

7. Follow-up interviews are as important as the first interview.
8. Learners should ask interviewees if there are other people to whom they can go for further information.
9. Educators need to help learners transcribe their interviews. A transcript means writing down exactly what is on the tape.

Note

1. Compiled by Jerry Hlabangane (for the History Workshop, University of Witwatersrand).

Contributors

Benedict Carton is a Professor of African History at George Mason University in the United States. Since the late 1980s, he has spent a lot of time living and researching in KwaZulu-Natal.

Philippe Denis is Professor of History of Christianity at the University of KwaZulu-Natal and the Director of the Sinomlando Centre for Oral History and Memory Work in Africa.

Sean Field is Director of the Centre for Popular Memory and Senior Lecturer in the Historical Studies Department at the University of Cape Town.

Cynthia Kros has been a member of the History Workshop for many years and is now the Head of the Division of Arts and Culture, Heritage and Management in the School of Arts, University of the Witwatersrand.

Mxolisi Mchunu is a doctoral candidate in History at the University of KwaZulu-Natal and is working as a researcher with the University of KwaZulu-Natal's Campbell Collections.

Radikobo Ntsimane is a researcher with the Sinomlando Centre for Oral History and Memory Work in Africa and is currently completing a doctoral degree in the History of Christianity at the University of KwaZulu-Natal.

Nicole Ulrich is a Ph.D. fellow at the Wits Institute for Social and Economic History (WISER) at the University of the Witwatersrand.

Louise Vis earned her Master's degree in Medical Science from the Nelson Mandela Medical School, University of KwaZulu-Natal. She has worked on a number of oral history projects related to public health in KwaZulu-Natal and is currently a practising nurse in the United States.

Julia Wells is Associate Professor of History in the History Department at Rhodes University. She is also a local government councillor and has served as a member of the National Heritage Council.

Select Bibliography

African Rights (Kigali, Rwanda). *A Wounded Generation: The Children Who Survived Rwanda's Genocide*. Discussion paper, no. 14 (2006), 5 (accessed via e-mail). See http://www.africanrights.org, accessed 27 May 2008.

Amdur, Robert. *Institutional Review Board Member Handbook*. Sudbury, MA: Jones & Bartlett, 2003.

Anderson, Kathryn and Dana C. Jack. 'Learning to Listen: Interviewing Techniques and Analyses'. In *Women's Words: The Feminist Practice of Oral History*, ed. Sherna Berger Gluck and Daphne Patai. New York: Routledge, 1991.

Ashforth, Adam. *Witchcraft, Violence, and Democracy in South Africa*. Chicago and London: Chicago University Press, 2005.

Barker, Pat. *Regeneration*. London: Penguin Books, 1991.

Bate, Stuart. *Inculturation and Healing*. Pietermaritzburg: Cluster Publications, 1995.

Beauchamp, Tom L. and James F. Childress. *Principles of Biomedical Ethics*. New York: Oxford University Press, 2001.

Berglund, Axel-Ivar. *Zulu Thought-Patterns and Symbolism*. London: Hurst and Co., 1976.

Bhavnani, Kum Kum. 'What's Power Got to Do with it? Empowerment and Social Research'. In *Deconstructing Social Psychology*, ed. Ian Parker and John Shotter. New York: Routledge, 1991.

Bickford-Smith, Vivian, Sean Field and Clive Glaser. 'The Western Cape Oral History Project: The 1990s'. *African Studies* 60, no. 1 (2001): 5–23.

Bonner, Philip. 'The Russians on the Reef, 1947–57: Urbanisation, Gang Warfare and Ethnic Mobilisation'. In *Apartheid's Genesis, 1935–1962*, ed. Philip Bonner, Peter Delius and Deborah Posel. Johannesburg: Witwatersrand University Press, 1993.

———. 'The History Workshop in South Africa, 1977–1994'. *Journal of American History* (December 1994): 977–85.

Bonner, Philip, Cynthia Kros, Peter Lekgoathi, Helen Ludlow, Sellow Mathabatha, Katie Mooney, Noor Nieftagodien, Nicole Ulrich, Ian Steenkamp and Wanga Tabata. 'Oral History: A Guide for Educators', pamphlet published by the Mpumalanga Department of Education, 2005. Available from the Mpumalanga Department of Education or from the History Workshop, http://web.wits.ac.

za/Academic/Humanities/SocialSciences/HistoryWorkshop/Training.htm, accessed 21 May 2008.

Borland, Katherine. ' "That's Not What I Said': Interpretive Conflict in Oral Narrative Research'. In *Women's Words: The Feminist Practice of Oral History*, ed. Sherna Berger Gluck and Daphne Patai. London: Routledge, 1991.

Bozzoli, Belinda. 'Intellectuals, Audiences and Histories: South African Experiences, 1978–1988'. *Radical History Review* 46, no. 7 (Winter 1990): 237–63. Also published in *History from South Africa: Alternative Visions and Practices*, ed. Joshua Brown, Patrick Manning, Karin Shapiro, Jon Wiener, Belinda Bozzoli and Peter Delius. Philadelphia: Temple University Press, 1991.

Bozzoli, Belinda and Peter Delius. 'Radical History and South African History'. In *History from South Africa: Alternative Visions and Practices*, ed. Joshua Brown, Patrick Manning, Karin Shapiro, Jon Wiener, Belinda Bozzoli and Peter Delius. Philadelphia: Temple University Press, 1991.

Bozzoli, Belinda, with Mmantho Nkotsoe. *Women of Phokeng: Consciousness, Life Strategy and Migrancy in South Africa, 1900–1983*. London: James Currey, 1991.

Bozzoli, Belinda, ed. *Class, Community and Conflict: South African Perspectives*. Johannesburg: Ravan Press, 1987.

Bradford, Helen. *A Taste of Freedom: The ICU in Rural South Africa, 1924–1930*. New Haven: Yale University Press, 1987.

Buthelezi, Mbongiseni. 'The Empire Talks Back: Challenging the Tyranny of Shaka and Zulu Kingdom Representations in Post-Apartheid KwaZulu-Natal'. In *Post Colonialism: South Africa*. Durban: AUETSA, SAVAL and SAACLALS Joint Congress, University of Natal, 2004.

Callinicos, Luli. *A People's History of South Africa. Vol. 2: Working Life, 1886–1940: Factories, Townships and Popular Culture on the Rand*. Johannesburg: Ravan Press, 1987.

———. 'Popular History in the Eighties'. In *History from South Africa: Alternative Visions and Practices*, ed. Joshua Brown, Patrick Manning, Karin Shapiro, Jon Wiener, Belinda Bozzoli and Peter Delius. Philadelphia: Temple University Press, 1991.

Carton, Benedict. *Blood from Your Children: The Colonial Origins of Generational Conflict*. Pietermaritzburg: University of Natal Press, 2000.

———. 'Fount of Deep Culture: Legacies of the James Stuart Archive in South African Historiography'. *History in Africa* 30 (2003): 87–106.

Casement, Patrick. *On Learning from the Patient*. London: Tavistock Publications, 1985.

Cobley, Alan. 'Does Social History Have a Future? The Ending of Apartheid and Recent Trends in South African Historiography'. *Journal of Southern African Studies* 27, no. 3 (September 2001): 613–25.

Crampton, Hazel. *The Sunburnt Queen*. Johannesburg: Jacana, 2004.

Cribb, Robert. 'Ethical Regulation and Humanities in Australia: Problems and Consequences'. *Monash Bioethics Review* 23, no. 3 (2004): 39–57.

Delius, Peter. *The Land Belongs to Us: The Pedi Polity, the Boers and the British in the Nineteenth-Century Transvaal.* Johannesburg: Ravan Press, 1983.

Delius, Peter, ed. *Mpumalanga: History and Heritage.* Pietermaritzburg: University of KwaZulu-Natal Press, 2007.

Delius, Peter and Clive Glaser. 'Sexual Socialisation in South Africa in an Historical Perspective'. *African Studies* 61, no. 1 (July 2002): 27–54.

Denis, Philippe. 'Healing the Wound of the Past: Oral History in Post-Apartheid South Africa'. In *Crossroads of History: Experience, Memory, Orality. XIth International Oral History Conference, Istanbul, 15–19 June 2000,* ed. Gunhan Danisman. Istanbul: Bogaziçi University, 2000.

———. 'Oral History in a Wounded Country'. In *Orality, Literacy and Colonialism in Southern Africa* (Semeia Studies, Vol. 46), ed. Jonathan Draper. Atlanta: Society of Biblical Literature; Pietermaritzburg: Cluster Publications, 2003.

———. ' "We Also Had to Live with Apartheid in Our Homes": Stories of Women in Sobantu, South Africa'. *Studia Historiae Ecclesiasticae* 30, no. 1 (June 2004): 151–67.

Denis, Philippe, ed. *Never Too Small to Remember: Memory Work and Resilience in the Times of AIDS.* Pietermaritzburg: Cluster Publications, 2005.

Denis, Philippe, Thulani Mlotshwa and George Mukuka, eds. *The Casspir and the Cross: Voices of Black Clergy in the Natal Midlands.* Pietermaritzburg: Cluster Publications, 1999.

Denis, Philippe and James Worthington, eds. *The Power of Oral History: Memory, Healing and Development. XIIth International Oral History Conference, Pietermaritzburg, 24–27 June 2002.* 4 vols. Pietermaritzburg: Sinomlando Centre, 2002.

Denzin, Norman and Yvonna Lincoln, eds. *Handbook of Qualitative Research.* Thousand Oaks, CA: Sage, 2000.

Department of Arts and Culture. 'White Paper on Arts, Culture and Heritage'. 1996. http://www.dac.gov.za/white_paper.htm, accessed 4 June 2007.

Dyer, Alison. 'Indigenous Rights'. Open Forum Paper, Monte Carlo, 3–6 November 1999. http://www.ficpi.org/library/montecarlo99/indigenous.html, accessed 10 May 2008.

Eisinger, Alison and Kirsten Senturia. 'Doing Community-Driven Research: A Description of Seattle Partners for Healthy Communities'. *Journal of Urban Health* 79, no. 3 (September 2001): 519–34.

Emanuel, Ezekiel J. 'Undue Inducement in Clinical Research in Developing Countries: Is it a Worry?' *The Lancet* 366 (2005): 336–40.

Emanuel, Ezekiel, David Wendler, Jack Killen and Christine Grady. 'What Makes Clinical Research in Developing Countries Ethical? The Benchmark of Ethical Research'. *Journal of Infectious Diseases* 189 (2004): 930–37.

Felman, Shosana and Dori Laub. *Testimony: Crises of Witnessing in Literature, Psychoanalysis and History*. London: Routledge, 1992.

Field, Sean. 'Remembering Experience, Interpreting Memory, Life Stories from Windermere'. *African Studies* 60, no. 1 (2001): 119–33.

———. 'Beyond "Healing": Trauma, Oral History and Regeneration'. *Oral History* 34, no. 1 (2006): 31–42.

Frisch, Michael, 'Oral History and *Hard Times*: A Review Essay'. In *The Oral History Reader*, ed. Robert Perks and Alistair Thomson. London: Routledge, 1998.

Fuze, Magema Magwaza. *The Black People and Whence They Came: A Zulu View*. Trans. H.C. Lugg and ed. A.T. Cope. Pietermaritzburg: University of Natal Press; Durban: Killie Campbell Africana Library, 1979.

Gasa, Nomboniso, ed. *Women in South African History: Basus'imbokodo, Bawel'imilambo – They Remove Boulders and Cross Rivers*. Cape Town: HSRC Press, 2006.

Gluck, Sherna Berger and Daphne Patai, eds. *Women's Words: The Feminist Practice of Oral History*. London: Routledge, 1991.

Gobodo-Madikizela, Pumla. *A Human Being Died that Night: A Story of Forgiveness*. Cape Town: David Philip, 2003.

Grady, Christine, Neal Dickert, Tom Jawets, Gary Gensler and Ezekiel Emanuel. 'An Analysis of US Practices of Paying Research Participants'. *Contemporary Clinical Trials* 26 (2005): 365–75.

Green, Anna. 'Individual Remembering and "Collective Memory": Theoretical Presuppositions and Contemporary Debates'. *Oral History* 32, no. 2 (2004): 35–44.

Grele, Ronald. 'Movement without Aim: Methodological and Theoretical Problems in Oral History'. In *Envelopes of Sound: The Art of Oral History*, 2nd ed., ed. Ronald Grele. New York: Praeger, 1991.

Grele, Ronald, ed. *The Art of Oral History*. 2nd ed. Chicago: Precedent Publishing, 1985.

———. *Envelopes of Sound: The Art of Oral History*. 2nd ed. New York: Praeger, 1991.

Gunner, Liz and Mafika Gwala, eds. *Musho: Zulu Popular Praises*. Johannesburg: Witwatersrand University Press, 1991.

Guy, Jeff. 'Gender Oppression in Southern Africa's Precapitalist Societies'. In *Women and Gender in Southern Africa to 1945*, ed. Cheryl Walker. Cape Town: David Philip, 1990.

Haddad, Beverley. *African Women's Theologies of Survival: Intersecting Faith, Feminisms, and Development*. Ph.D. dissertation, University of Natal, 2000.

Hamilton, Carolyn. ' "Living by Fluidity": Oral Histories, Material Custodies and the Politics of Archiving'. In *Refiguring the Archive*, ed. Carolyn Hamilton, Verne Harris, Jane Taylor, Michele Pickover, Graeme Reid and Razia Saleh. Cape Town: David Philip, 2002.

———. 'Emerging Themes and Trends, Opportunities and Challenges'. Concluding paper of a workshop organised by the South African History Workshop and the Rosa Luxemburg Foundation, Johannesburg, 16–18 November 2006. http://www.public-conversations.org.za/pdf/archival_platform_paper.pdf, accessed 4 June 2007.

Hammond-Tooke, William David. 'N.J. Van Warmelo and the Ethnological Section: A Memoir'. *African Studies* 54, no. 1 (1995): 119–28.

Harrits, Kirsten Folke and Ditte Scharnberg. 'We Ourselves are History: An Oral History Project in Denmark'. In *Proceedings of the 12th IOHA Conference, Pietermaritzburg, 24–27 June 2002*. Vol. 3. Pietermaritzburg: Sinomlando Centre, 2002.

Henige, David. *Oral Historiography*. London: Longman, 1982.

Hirson, Denis. *White Scars: On Reading and Rites of Passage*. Johannesburg: Jacana, 2006.

Hofmeyr, Isabel. *'We Spend Our Years as a Tale that is Told': Oral Historical Narrative in a South African Chiefdom*. Johannesburg: Witwatersrand University Press, 1994.

Horrell, Muriel. *Group Areas: The Emerging Pattern with Illustrative Examples from the Transvaal*. Johannesburg: South African Institute of Race Relations, 1966.

Huerta, Grace and Leslie Flemmer. 'Using Student-Generated Oral History Research in the Secondary Classroom'. *Social Studies* 91, no. 3 (2000): 110–15.

Inglis, David. *Culture and Everyday Life*. New York: Routledge, 2005.

Jones, David. 'Distressing Histories and Unhappy Interviewing'. *Oral History* 26, no. 2 (1998), 49–56.

Joutard, Philippe. *Ces voix qui nous viennent du passé*. Paris: Hachette, 1983.

Kanyoro, Musimbi. *Introducing Feminist Cultural Hermeneutics: An African Perspective*. London: Sheffield, 2000.

Keegan, Tim. *Facing the Storm: Portraits of Black Lives in South Africa*. London: Zed Press, 1988.

Kendall, Limakatso A., ed. *Basali! Stories by and about Women in Lesotho*. Pietermaritzburg: University of Natal Press, 1995.

Khoza, Brian. 'Crossing the Great Eye Contact Divide'. *The Witness*, 30 January 2008.

Klein, Kerwin Lee. 'On the Emergence of Memory in Historical Discourse'. *Representations, Special Issue: Grounds for Remembering* 69 (Winter 2000): 127–50.

Kurasawa, Fuyuki. 'A Message in a Bottle: Bearing Witness as a Mode of Ethico-Political Practice'. http://research.yale.edu/ccs/papers/kurasawa_witnessing.pdf, accessed 1 February 2005.

La Capra, Dominick. *History and Memory after Auschwitz*. Ithaca: Cornell University Press, 1998.

———. *Writing History, Writing Trauma*. Baltimore: Johns Hopkins University Press, 2001.

———. *History in Transit: Experience, Identity, Critical Theory*. Ithaca: Cornell University Press, 2004.

La Hausse, Paul. 'Oral History and South African Historians'. *Radical History Review* 46, no. 7 (1990): 346–56.

———. 'Oral Historians and South African Historians'. In *History from South Africa: Alternative Visions and Practices*, ed. Joshua Brown, Patrick Manning, Karin Shapiro, Jon Wiener, Belinda Bozzoli and Peter Delius. Philadelphia: Temple University Press, 1991.

Ladner, Joyce, ed. *The Death of White Sociology*. New York: Random House, 1973.

Lawson, Lesley and Helene Perold. *Working Women: A Portrait of South African Black Women Workers*. Johannesburg: Sached Trust/Ravan Press, 1985.

Lekgoathi, Peter. 'Voices of Our Past: Oral Testimony and Teaching History'. Keynote address delivered to History Workshop's annual workshop for teachers, 2003. In *Educator's Guide to the UNESCO General History of Africa (for the FET Curriculum)*, ed. J. Bam and C. Dyer. Cape Town: New Africa Education for the Ministry of Education, 2004.

Lihamba, Amandina, Fulata L. Moyo, Mugyabuso M. Mulokozi, Naomi L. Shitemi and Saïda Yahya-Othman, eds. *Women Writing Africa: The Eastern Region*. New York: The Feminist Press, 2007.

Luthuli, Albert. *Let My People Go*. Glasgow: Collins, 1962.

Macklin, Ruth. ' "Due" and "Undue" Inducements: On Paying Money to Research Subjects'. *IRB: A Review of Human Subjects* 3, no. 5 (May 1981): 1–6.

Magubane, Bernard, Phil Bonner and Noor Nieftagodien. 'The Turn to Armed Struggle'. In *The Road to Democracy in South Africa, Vol. 1: 1960–1970*, South African Democracy Education Trust. Cape Town: Zebra Press, 2004.

Magwaza, Thenjiwe, Yonah Seleti and Mpilo Pearl Sithole, eds. *Freedom Sown in Blood': Memories of the Impi Yamakhanda, An Indigenous Knowledge Systems Perspective*. Thohoyandou: Ditlou Publishers, 2006.

Mamdani, Mahmood. *Citizen and Subject: Contemporary Africa and the Legacy of Late Colonialism*. Princeton, NJ: Princeton University Press, 1996.

Mchunu, Mxolisi. 'Discipline, Respect and Ethnicity: A Study of the Changing Patterns of Fatherhood of Three Generations of Zulu Fathers and Sons in KwaShange, Inadi, Vulindlela Area of Pietermaritzburg, KwaZulu-Natal, from the 1930s to the 1990s'. Master's thesis, University of KwaZulu-Natal, Durban, 2005.

McNally, Richard. *Remembering Trauma*. Cambridge, MA: Belknap Press/Harvard University Press, 2003.

Minister, Kristina. 'A Feminist Frame for the Oral History Interview'. In *Women's Words: The Feminist Practice of Oral History*, ed. Sherna Berger Gluck and Daphne Patai. London: Routledge, 1991.

Minkley, Gary and Ciraj Rassool. 'Orality, Memory and Social History in South Africa'. In *Negotiating the Past: The Making of Memory in South Africa*, ed. Sarah Nuttall and Carli Coetzee. Cape Town: Oxford University Press, 1998.

Mthethwa, Dingani. 'Two Bulls in One Kraal: Local Politics, "Zulu History", and

Heritage Tourism in Kosi Bay, KwaZulu-Natal'. In *Zulu Identities: Being Zulu, Past and Present*, ed. Benedict Carton, John Laband and Jabulani Sithole. Pietermaritzburg: University of KwaZulu-Natal Press; London: Christopher Hurst; New York: Columbia University Press, 2008.

Neuenschwander, John A. *Oral History and the Law*. 3rd ed. Pennsylvania: Oral History Association, 2002.

Niehaus, Isak. *Witchcraft, Power and Politics: Exploring the Occult in the South African Lowveld*. London: Pluto Press, 2001.

Ntsimane, Radikobo. 'Dominant Masculinities within the Zion Christian Church: A Preliminary Investigation'. *Journal of Constructive Theology* 12, no. 1 (July 2006): 27–37.

Ntsoane, Otsile. 'Intellectual Property Rights and Natural Resources: Some Case Studies amongst Arts and Farming Communities in the North-West Province, South Africa'. Paper prepared for the International Workshop on Intellectual Property Rights and Indigenous Knowledge Systems, University of Botswana, 26–28 November 2003.

Nuttall, Tim and John Wright. 'Exploring beyond History with a Capital "H"'. *Current Writing* 10, no. 2 (1998): 38–61.

Odendaal, Andre. 'Developments in Popular History in the Western Cape in the 1980s'. In *History from South Africa: Alternative Visions and Practices*, ed. Joshua Brown, Patrick Manning, Karin Shapiro, Jon Wiener, Belinda Bozzoli and Peter Delius. Philadelphia: Temple University Press, 1991.

Oral History Association (OHA). 'Oral History Evaluation Guidelines, Pamphlet No. 3'. http://www.dickinson.edu/organizations/oha/pub_eg.html, accessed 21 June 2006.

Parle, Julie. 'The Voice of History? Archives, Ethics and Historians'. *Journal of Natal and Zulu History* 24–25 (2006–2007): 164–87.

Penyak, Lee and Pamela Duray. 'Oral History and Problematic Questions Promote Issue Centered Education'. *Social Studies* 90, no. 2 (1999): 68–71.

Perks, Robert and Alistair Thomson, eds. *The Oral History Reader*. 2nd ed. London: Routledge, 2006.

Phiri, Isabel and Sarojini Nadar, eds. *African Women, Religion, and Health*. Pietermaritzburg: Cluster Publications, 2006.

Portelli, Alessandro. 'Uchronic Dreams: Working Class Memory and Possible Worlds'. In *The Myths We Live By*, ed. Raphael Samuel and Paul Thompson. London: Routledge, 1990.

————. *The Death of Luigi Trastulli and Other Stories: Form and Meaning in Oral History*. Albany: State University of New York Press, 1991.

————. *The Battle of Valle Giulia: Oral History and the Art of Dialogue*. Madison: University of Wisconsin Press, 1997.

————. 'What Makes Oral History Different?' In *The Oral History Reader*, ed. Robert Perks and Alistair Thomson. London: Routledge, 1998.

Posel, Deborah and Graeme Simpson, eds. *Commissioning the Past: Understanding South Africa's Truth and Reconciliation Commission*. Johannesburg: Witwatersrand University Press, 2002.

Radstone, Suzannah. 'Working with Memory: An Introduction'. In *Memory and Methodology*, ed. Suzannah Radstone. Oxford and New York: Berg, 2000.

Reisberg, Daniel and Paula Hertel, eds. *Memory and Emotion*. Oxford: Oxford University Press, 2004.

Ritchie, Donald. 'Institutional Review Boards and Oral History'. *Oral History Association Newsletter* 35 (Fall 2001).

———. *Doing Oral History: A Practical Guide*. 2nd ed. New York: Oxford University Press, 2003.

Rogers, Kim Lacy, Selma Leydesdorff and Graham Dawson, eds. *Trauma and Life Stories: International Perspectives*. London: Routledge, 1999.

Roper, Michael. 'Analysing the Analysed: Transference and Counter-Transference in the Oral History Encounter'. *Oral History* 31, no. 2 (2003): 20–32.

Rosenzweig, Roy and David Thelen. *The Presence of the Past: Popular Uses of History in American Life*. New York: Columbia University Press, 1998.

Ross, William David. *The Good and the Right*. Oxford: Oxford University Press, 1930.

Rousseau, Nicole. 'Popular History in South Africa in the 1980s: The Politics of Production'. Master's thesis, University of the Western Cape, 1994.

Shopes, Linda. 'Institutional Review Boards Have a Chilling Effect on Oral History'. *AHA Perspectives* 38, no. 6 (September 2000). http://www.historians.org/perspectives/issues/2000/0009/0009vie1.cfm, accessed 10 May 2008.

Sithole, Mpilo Pearl. 'Genealogies of the Royal AmaZondi of Ngome'. In *'Freedom Sown in Blood': Memories of the Impi Yamakhanda: An Indigenous Knowledge Systems Perspective*, ed. Thenjiwe Magwaza, Yonah Seleti and Mpilo Pearl Sithole. Thohoyandou: Ditlou Publishers, 2006.

Slim, Hugo and Paul Thompson. *Listening for a Change: Oral Testimony and Development*. London: Panos Publications, 1993.

Sommer, Barbara and Mary Kay Quinlan. *Oral History Manual*. New York: Alta Mira Press, 2002.

Stolorow, Robert. 'An Intersubjective View of Self Psychology'. *Psychoanalytic Dialogues* 5, no. 3 (1995): 393–99.

South African Democracy Education Trust (SADET). *The Road to Democracy in South Africa, Vol. 1: 1960–1970*. Cape Town: Zebra Press, 2004.

———. *The Road to Democracy in South Africa, Vol. 2: 1970–1980*. Pretoria: University of South Africa Press, 2006.

Stuart, James. *A History of the Zulu Rebellion 1906*. London: Macmillan, 1913.

Tedlock, Dennis. 'Oral History as Poetry'. In *The Art of Oral History*, 2nd ed., ed. Ronald Grele. Chicago: Precedent Publishing, 1985.

Thompson, Paul. *The Voice of the Past: Oral History*. 3rd ed. New York: Oxford University Press, 2000.

———. 'Reconciling Recent Oral Tradition with Old Documents: Bhambatha and His Family'. Paper read at the second conference of the Oral History Society of South Africa, Richards Bay, 7–10 November 2006.

Thomson, Alistair. *Anzac Memories: Living with the Legend*. Melbourne: Oxford University Press, 1994.

———. 'Dancing through the Memory of Our Movement: Four Paradigmatic Revolutions in Oral History'. Paper presented at the fourteenth conference of the International Oral History Association, Sydney, July 2006.

Tonkin, Elizabeth. *Narrating Our Past: The Social Construction of Oral History*. Cambridge: Cambridge University Press, 1992.

Townsend, Robert, Carl Ashley, Mériam Belli, Richard Bond and Elizabeth Fairhead. 'Oral History and Review Boards: Little Gain and More Pain'. *Perspectives* 44, no. 2 (February 2006). http://www.historians.org/Perspectives/issues/2006/0602/0602new1.cfm, accessed 10 May 2008.

Townsend, Robert and Mériam Belli. 'Oral History and IRBs: Caution Urged as Rule Interpretations Vary Widely'. *Perspectives* 42, no. 9 (December 2004). http://www.historians.org/perspectives/issues/2004/0412/0412new4.cfm, accessed 10 May 2008.

Van Onselen, Charles. 'The Reconstruction of a Rural Life from Oral Testimony: Critical Notes on the Methodology Employed in the Study of a Black South African Sharecropper'. *Journal of Peasant Studies* 20, no. 3 (1993): 494–514.

———. *The Seed is Mine: The Life of Kas Maine, a South African Sharecropper 1894–1985*. Cape Town: David Philip, 1996.

Vansina, Jan. *Oral Tradition as History*. London: James Currey, 1985.

Vilakazi, Absalom. *Zulu Transformation: A Study of the Dynamics of Social Change*. Pietermaritzburg: University of Natal Press, 1965.

Ward, Alan. 'Oral History Society Ethical Guidelines'. In *Is Your Oral History Legal and Ethical?* http://www.oralhistory.org.uk/ethics, accessed 10 May 2008.

Wassenaar, Douglas. 'Ethical Issues in Social Science Research'. In *Research in Practice: Applied Methods for the Social Sciences*, ed. Martin Terreblanche, Kevin Durrheim and Desmond Painter. Cape Town: University of Cape Town Press, 2006.

Webb, Colin de B. and John Wright, eds. *The James Stuart Archive of Recorded Oral Evidence Relating to the History of the Zulu and Neighbouring Peoples*. 5 vols. Pietermaritzburg: University of Natal Press, 1976–2001.

White, Luise, Stephan Miescher and David Cohen, eds. *African Words, African Voices: Critical Practices in Oral History*. Bloomington: Indiana University Press, 2001.

Willis, Roy. *The Interpretation of Symbolism*. London: Malaby Press, 1975.

Yow, Valerie. ' "Do I Like Them Too Much?" Effects of the Oral History Interview on the Interviewer and Vice Versa'. In *The Oral History Reader*, 2nd ed., ed. Robert Perks and Alistair Thomson. London: Routledge, 2006.

Index

190